10 STORIES OF STRONG LIVING

True Fitness Begins in Your Heart

FOREWORD BY
TODD DURKIN

PUBLISHING GROUP

PUBLISHED BY
SCRIPTOR PUBLISHING GROUP

TABLE OF CONTENTS

Foreword *Todd Durkin* 1

Chapter 1: Wake Up! Your Life is Now! *Jill Ruth Rooks* 8

Chapter 2: Believe in Yourself *Tim Rhode* 23

Chapter 3: Rise Up! *Preston Smith* 42

Chapter 4: Find Your Voice *Amanda Mittleman* 52

Chapter 5: Fueling the Fire Within *Christine Parker* 68

Chapter 6: Mind, Body...Game *Christa Pryor* 83

Chapter 7: Decade Thinking *Lisa Berman* 101

Chapter 8: Living Between Extremes *Kelli O'Brien Corasanti* 117

Chapter 9: Creating a World-Class Mindset:
How to Control Your Own Fate *Greg Justice* 133

Chapter 10: Overachieve For The Life You Want *Ralph Roberts* . 146

FOREWORD

by Todd Durkin

Being a mentor and coach is one of the most important roles and responsibilities in my life. As someone whose purpose is to create, motivate, and inspire people to greatness, and create IMPACT every day, it brings me tremendous pride and joy when I see people who I have coached, mentored, trained, and spent years working with do BIG things.

As a performance coach, trainer, speaker, and business owner, I have had the opportunity to work with some of the world's best athletes and executives from NFL MVPs, Super Bowl champions and MVPs, MLB and NBA All-Stars, and Olympic gold medalists to the uber successful entrepreneur who is worth billions of dollars. As a Mastermind coach, I have also had the opportunity to mentor, coach, and work with the best of the best in the sports-training world and health and fitness industry.

And one thing is common with the great ones. All the athletes, clients, coaches, and fitness professionals and entrepreneurs I have had the opportunity to mentor and coach share one thing in common: a deep desire in their heart to maximize their potential, be the best version of themselves, and fulfill their life's purpose. And that fires me up!

I have often said, "We all have a life worth telling a story about . . . What's your story?"

You, my friends reading this masterpiece you are holding in your hands, have 10 incredible "stories" from 10 of the most amazing, passionate, and loving human beings you will ever meet. EVER. They are the best of the best. And their stories and lessons will help motivate and inspire you to craft up your best life also.

So that you completely understand my deep relationship with all 10 of these authors, I have had the incredible opportunity to connect, coach, and be a part of each of their lives for many years. I have watched them grow. I have watched their dreams expand and unfold.

I believe when you read this book and glean its top themes and lessons, the following 5 things will happen for you:

1. **You will strengthen your BELIEF in yourself.** With all the champions and entrepreneurs I work with, so much of success is between the ears. I often tell my clients and athletes to "get your mind right." In this book, you will not only learn about the importance of mindset, but you will strengthen your own mindset and beliefs also.

2. **You will use fear to propel you, not paralyze you.** Fear is a real emotion that everyone experiences. Instead of having fear rob you of your dreams and destiny, you want to use fear as a motivator to accomplish the things you desire.

   If you have fear in your life, run AT the fear, not FROM the fear. You will learn that with time, effort, persistence, and dedication your fear will soon be triumphed.

   Remember, "Fear, frustration, and failure are overcome with faith, fortitude, forward-thinking, and follow-through." Thank you, Wayne Cotton.

2

3. **You will dream bigger than ever before.** Dreams stir your emotions and fuel your passion. The life stories, lessons, and wisdom shared in this book will certainly help motivate and inspire you to dream big and keep grinding.

4. **You will be inspired to have more grit, determination, and heart than ever before.**

   It's important to dream and have a great vision of what you want out of life. But it's even more important to match your dream with a tenacious work ethic, mental toughness in the face of adversity, and the grit necessary to overcome any challenge or obstacle that you may face.

5. **Your mind, body, and soul will be STRONGER, and you will be ready to share your message and "voice."** If your body is not strong, you can't function at your best. If your mind is weak, there is no possible way you can tap into the mindset necessary to build what you want. If your spirit is not singing, you can't soar in the stratosphere like you desire.

   The words, stories, and lessons in this book will help you develop the STRENGTH necessary to optimize your full personal and professional potential, develop your voice, and spread your message and purpose.

6. **And then some.** I always include "and then some" in anything I do. And these 10 authors always do the same in all they do. We are cut out of the same cloth. And so are you. That's why you're reading this book.

Enjoy this read like a fine wine. You can sip it slowly and take your time by reading just one chapter a day for 10 days straight. Or you can be so fired up and ready for "strong living" that you read it in one sitting.

Either way, know that you can come back to it, revisit the stories, and get re-inspired with profound wisdom at any time.

Lastly, I want to thank each of the authors for doing such an amazing job with their chapters: Jill Ruth-Rooks, Tim Rhode, Preston Smith, Christine Parker, Ralph Roberts, Lisa Berman, Christa Pryor, Amanda Mittleman, Kelli O'Brien Corasanti, and Greg Justice.

I must tell you that I got choked up reading this book. Why? First, because it has such heart-felt love, compassion, and genuine care behind each and every word. Second, because I know that each of the authors has a special story and had the courage to share their story with so many people. And lastly, because I know the IMPACT that their messages, stories, and this book can create. And to me, that's what makes me tick.

I have always said that you want to surround yourself with "thoroughbreds and not donkeys." These 10 authors are the best of the best "thoroughbreds" out there, and I am blessed to have them in my life.

My friends, as you get ready to dive into the ***10 Stories of Strong Living: True Fitness Begins in Your Heart***, I also want to thank YOU.

I want to thank YOU for what you do. You matter.

I want to thank YOU for being a positive light in the world. It's a choice. You either spread positivity and do great works for others, or you stay self-absorbed in your own world. Serve others, give back more than you receive, and keep shining. There is too much negativity in the world, and we can NOT stand for that. Thank you for being a difference-maker!

I want to thank YOU for having a dream and be willing to go get it. It's going to take hard work, dedication, overcoming adversity, and surrounding yourself with the right people, but thank you for keeping your dream alive. Now, go get it!

4

Lastly, I want to thank YOU for reading this extraordinary book. It's going to make a big difference in your life and help you on your journey to live a life worth telling a story about. I can't wait to hear your feedback on the book and see how it makes a difference in your life.

Share it with your family.

Share it with your colleagues and coworkers.

Share it with your teammates.

And share it with strangers.

Most of all, LIVE IT every day and BE STRONG.

It's time to get reading!

Continue to strive for excellence, dream BIG, and create WOW and IMPACT in all you do.

Much love and much STRENGTH.

— Todd Durkin

About Todd Durkin

Todd Durkin is an internationally recognized fitness trainer, coach, author, and speaker who works with some of the highest level athletes in the NFL, MLB, MMA, and Olympics. Todd was a featured trainer on NBC's *STRONG* last year (produced by Sylvester Stallone) and owns Fitness Quest 10 in San Diego, an award-winning gym that has been named a Top 10 Gym in the US 5 years in a row by *Men's Health*. He leads a team of 38 employees and runs a Mastermind Group for hundreds of fitness professionals.

Todd is the lead training advisor for Under Armour and has been voted a "Top 100 Most Influential People in Health & Fitness" with Tony Robbins, Dr. Oz, and Michelle Obama. He will be honored in July 2017 as the recipient of the Jack LaLanne Award, for creating lasting legacy and impact in the fitness world.

His Amazon bestselling *The WOW BOOK—52 Ways to Motivate Your Mind, Inspire Your Soul, and Create WOW in Your Life* is creating massive WOW in the universe. Also Todd delivers motivational keynotes and programs worldwide. Todd is a man who lives by the words *passion*, *purpose*, and *impact*.

Todd is married and has 3 kids, ages 14, 11, and 9.

Todd Durkin, MA, CSCS

Owner, Fitness Quest 10

Author, *The WOW BOOK* and *The IMPACT Body Plan*

Top 100 Most Influential People in Health & Fitness

www.fitnessquest10.com

Instagram: @ToddDurkin

Facebook: @ToddDurkinFQ10

CHAPTER 1

WAKE UP! YOUR LIFE IS NOW!

by Jill Ruth Rooks

We have all watched that moment in the movies when you receive a phone call that someone you love has been taken by ambulance to the hospital. When you arrive, you are brought into a room with a doctor who begins by saying, "We did everything we could, but we could not save his life."

That moment happened to me on August 14, 2006.

It felt like I had been punched in the gut. It took my breath away and left me speechless. "This can't be happening to me." Everything went numb, and time stood still.

I was with my mom and my husband, the three of us receiving the news together. Disbelief and yet a simultaneous sensation that this was really happening took over.

He was my guide. He was my hero.

My dad.

"Do you want to see him?" they asked.

Of course, I wanted to see my dad. My dad, my hero, the funny, jovial, easy-going, large man who was at my house just two days before. That day we were doing what he loved, eating and being together with family. He and Brendan, my six-year old son, were chasing each other around. He and Natalie, my four-year old, who was delighted by his efforts to tickle her, were having breakfast together.

Yes, I wanted to see my dad.

They brought us into a room where his body lay. His gym shoes were on. That was all I could think, "His gym shoes are on. He is in his workout clothes. He is okay." I held his hand. I searched for his pulse. I swore I could feel it as I squeezed harder and harder. If only I could send my pulse into his arm and wake him up.

Something else tugged at my heart. He looked peaceful. He had been taken from this world at the young age of 64 to a better place. His heart simply gave its last beat. I found myself pleading with God, "Please take him into heaven, Dear God. Please forgive him. He has been the best father a girl could ask for."

I thought of his friends for whom he cared so deeply, who had been taken before him. I thought of his brothers whose lives he mourned, whose memories he cherished. He was a storyteller, and he loved to talk. People who shaped him, whom he talked about and cared for, came flooding across my mind. He loved hard. He cared deeply. He took pride in his work. He went to the gym every day for as long as I could remember. He told stories of his gym friends, of his customers, of his grandchildren, of grocery store sales and coupons, and of what he had for dinner.

As my dad went to sleep for the final time, I woke up.

We are all products of where we have been, whom we have been influenced by, and the people we surround ourselves with. Early in life, we are given our family, childhood neighbors, and school friends. Later in life, we have the opportunity to make conscious choices about whom we want to surround ourselves with. The energy we carry attracts the energy of others similar to ourselves, and we create our environment. This is all done without much thought, as though we are asleep.

Over ten years ago, I made a conscious decision to surround myself with others on the same mission. I did not know at the time that my mission was to be a carrier of contagious positive energy, but I knew I had a mission to be present for people and to somehow play a small part in making this world a better place. I became conscious of my calling when I held onto life as dearly as I held onto death. It was then that I knew it was time for me to wake up.

I had shoes to fill and a role to take on. Clifford Ruth, my father, was my guide. From him, I learned the lineage of life, of love, of character, of the beauty of connections and relationships. It seemed that in his death, I woke up to my role to carry on his ability to connect to the world in which he lived and served. I learned not only from my dad but also from the people who shaped him. He was a storyteller. He lived life fully. He took risks, and he knew how to say, "Yes." His parents both died when he was in high school. He went to Waynesburg College, played college football and baseball. He spoke of his older siblings and their spouses who looked out for him, of coaches and teachers who taught him and with whom he lived. In his community, there were individuals who wove themselves into the fabric of his being. Their fibers made him who he was, and he became more fully himself through their love.

In looking at my dad's life, I admire how much he cared. He thought of others first, and he sought to please with little tokens of love. Chocolate was one of his favorite ways to show that he loved me. I do not remember the words, "I love you," spoken, but I do remember a lot of chocolate.

Time was his other gift. He spent time with us. Out in our New Jersey backyard as kids, we learned how to run football patterns. We learned the basketball game HORSE, and we were taught to say yes to trying new things. He served. There were four kids, and we were always recruited to be the "behind-the-scenes" help for the numerous pancake breakfasts and Knights of Columbus dinners. It made me feel special to be a part of his community.

All of this ended on that day in August of 2006. When a parent passes on, the child receives a piece of their heart containing the energy and language of that person. I am sure that the thread, the vibrations that the life force holds, continues on. When it is but a memory, a "feeling," it is like an eggshell—extremely fragile and yet wonderfully resilient. It is a container for life.

For someone unaware of what a gift it is to carry that intangible energy, it could be daunting to figure out what fills the place of the one who has left. When my dad left this world, I realized that it was my gift, a piece of his heart, which I was given. It is his life force and energy that I must use to carry on his story and share his message to the world. I am called to love as he loved.

This awareness woke me up.

What is life for, if not to serve? I learned that from my dad.

What is life for, if not to use the gifts we have been given? I learned that from my faith in God.

What is life for, if not to leave a little bit of ourselves in the hearts of others? I learned that from my family, my friends, and my community, as well as from a lot of threads, which have been woven into the tapestry of my story.

"To whom much is given, much is required" (Luke 12:48). This rings in my ears often. "Much is required" is the work of carrying my own gift, but more than that—using it to bring light to the world and shining it on others to illuminate their gifts. What can I do for others? How can I serve you?

When I woke up and realized the gift my dad left me, it changed my life. When I share this gift, I weave a piece of everyone I have met and have learned from into my being, into my story, into our story. Not only does that keep my dad and those who have made an impact on me very much alive, but I can pass this onto my children as well.

There is so much for the world to learn as our threads weave into the tapestry of generations to come. We are all a piece of something so much bigger than any one of us alone. We are connected to the world and to the universe, and a piece of us will carry on forever.

Without this interconnectedness, life is flat. There are too many people who are still asleep, unaware of the beauty that exists within and around, too afraid to open up, and maybe, also, too afraid to listen. The emotions that unfold, the connections that flow, and the sharing that takes place are all reflections of **strong living**: the courage to connect, to love, and to serve.

To go out on a limb with another human being and to simultaneously become vulnerable in order to become alive is what I believe makes a strong life. If you can do this, you can do anything. If you are not doing this, then the time is NOW. Wake up! Go out and take action by loving more, serving more, and connecting more!

If you are not sure how, then these stories will show you. This is a rare and precious opportunity to see inside the hearts and souls of the bearers of these stories. If you look closely enough, you will see our stories begin to unravel. Welcome to the journey of love in action!

Unconditional Love

My friend Phil will be celebrating his 100th birthday in 2017. I go to his house, and we practice T'ai Chi together.

When we first started working together, Phil was 92. He asked if I would train him so that he could continue getting up and down with ease. He is a retired physician, World War II veteran, father of 8, and former Associate Dean of UCLA Medical School. When someone is a high performer, they cannot suddenly shut down the practices that made them that way, and yet for Phil, his peer group, those who understand him, are slowly disappearing. It is a lonely place. I could sense his frustration with life, and depression was setting in.

I understood that a worthwhile life for Phil was one in which he kept moving, so I suggested T'ai Chi. His mind was sharp, and he was skeptical, so he asked, "How can I do that?"

My hope was to go to the root of movement, so I explained to him, "It starts with our breath. When we breathe, energy flows, and we move."

He did not like the answer I gave him. Phil wanted to stay strong, but initially he didn't see the connection between T'ai Chi and strength. I explained that we did not need weights to keep him strong. He didn't understand, but he didn't give up either.

He said, "You know, most people would not get this."

I responded, "I know. You are not most people."

I encouraged him, while we moved, to picture something he loved, an energy force. For him, that energy was Sophie, his dog of years ago. She was a Great Pyrenees.

Again, I told Phil, "When we breathe, energy flows, and we move. As we connect with that energy, we can see Sophie."

13

Phil's expression changed when he saw Sophie, giving his eyes a depth I had not seen before.

Phil can now summon Sophie anytime he wants. With her, his chi is strong, he is strong, and he can move. Unconditional love is like that. It feeds us. For Phil, Sophie is unconditional love. She looked into his eyes and saw Phil, exactly as he was. There is nothing superficial about Sophie.

When we enable this type of meditation into our daily life practices, we become free of life's stressors and pains. Clarity appears, and we are awake. We just have to see it. It is the space between the thoughts. It is your Sophie, your unconditional love. We are all capable of receiving it. If we can receive it, we can give it too.

Just as I keep my dad's spirit and energy with me, Phil keeps Sophie's close to him. It takes courage to let go of something we love so dearly, but with time, as we accept the temporal loss, we discover that the essence of the soul, and the energy of the thread we are left with, is what life is about. We fight to hold onto what we have lost, not realizing that when we have the courage to let go and the faith to look through a different lens, we gain a new relationship that is deeper than ever before. It will stand the test of time and distance. As my dad and Phil taught me, unconditional love never dies.

Life Is Funny

My friend Audrey once told me, "It's funny how life turns pages and forgets to help the person whom it left behind." I have not been able to let go of that thought. Does life leave us behind or do we give up on life? When Audrey and I are together, we often have more questions than we have answers. That's when she says, "What the hell, Charlie?"

Audrey, born in 1933, is not your typical client. She was sure she was in the wrong place at our first meeting. I had helped her nephew with his golf game and helped his father through the last few months of his life. He wanted me to help Aunt Audrey. Ironically, she is the one who helped me! Time with her is like being with an old friend you knew once upon a time.

For a tiny woman, her presence is huge. She loves her Armenian heritage. She is proud and stands straight, disdainful of the "others" in the "old folks' home" who rely on walkers and wheelchairs. Audrey loves reading the wall quotes and motivational sayings we have in The Energy Lab. Her favorite is "When was the last time you did something for the first time?"

One day she noticed, "You are always stronger than you think you are." She asked me, "Do you believe that?"

I said, "Of course."

Early in life, Audrey was told, "You can't do that backbend. Your spine is too long." There was a "mean neighbor" who told her to get out of the tree she was climbing because "you will fall down." For her, the idea of "being stronger than you think you are" contradicted many lifelong beliefs. As Audrey stands the test of time, she recognizes the capacity of her strength of character and will. Her strength was never questioned until she started sharing stories with me. By sharing her stories and seeing herself in a new light, she began to see her own strength.

After two years, Audrey had some health complications and was moved to an Alzheimer's facility. I continue to visit her. What she and I have both learned from life inside this facility is a book unto itself. For now "Life is funny" keeps her going. In our visits, we focus on the stories and the people who made her who she is. Plus, we are keeping her memories turning and her brain busy.

Marianne Williamson says, "Something very beautiful happens to people when their world has fallen apart; a humility, a nobility, a higher intelligence emerges at just the point when our knees hit the floor." Audrey struggles every day. I watch the energy of her life ebb and flow like the tides. What Audrey has discovered as a means of preservation, and what I have learned from her, is that the true test of strength is the courage to let go.

It sometimes makes me sad to listen to Audrey observe life around her and realize that she can no longer make her own decisions. While there are moments when she is not at peace with letting go of her independence, she has ironically let go of it in other ways, creating a different world for herself. One of the roles she has appointed herself is feeding the gentleman in the wheelchair who sits beside her at meals. He cannot feed himself. Before her life changed, she had no patience for others in wheelchairs and walkers. It seems that part of the beauty of her letting go is her acceptance of her circumstance and that of other people's. She takes pride in being his helper. Her empathy and compassion for the other residents is remarkable. At the same time, she shares her dreams with me about the women's clothing store she is going to open. She recognizes that she is "bored" and needs something to do. She wants to be able to work again. We brainstorm about what her store will look like, and we named it "Audrey's Place."

I told Audrey the other day that she is still that strong woman even though she does not know all the answers anymore. She said, "Yes, but I think that being strong is not always so good." To see this woman who had all the answers one day realize that she doesn't anymore is a lesson in vulnerability. "What the hell, Charlie?" is sometimes all we can say or do, and that is enough.

What a humbling experience life is, growing old and letting go, and yet, how liberating. The lesson that we do not need to have all the answers and can carry on, making the most of what we are given, sets us free.

It can be a burden to be great. It can be a burden to be strong. To be strong is an expectation that when not met, puts a condition on love. Strong living is the ability to love, the ability to squeeze the heart; and the heart, the vessel of emotions, recognizes that the ability to feel love and to feel joy is only possible because of the ability to feel sorrow and despair. We cannot have one without the other. When I am with Audrey, the mystery of life and the duality of the heart epitomize strong living. Audrey is the reminder that it is not the load that breaks us, but how we carry it.

"They Didn't Know We Were Seeds."

There is a Mexican proverb that says, "They tried to bury us. They didn't know we were seeds." I think of resiliency, tenacity, grit, and the uncommon ability to rise up. I think of a few "warriors" who have shown me that they are, indeed, seeds. It is not something that can be spoken. It is something that must be done. Actions speak louder than words, and I am fortunate to witness it first-hand.

It intrigues me to see the response in others when people with disabilities, who fight cancer, or who endure other unfortunate circumstances, put themselves on the line. I have worked with many clients who live these stories, and although each of their experiences is different, one of the most beautiful things I have witnessed is that they do not go through it alone. All of these clients are part of a "duo" consisting of themselves and another person who lifts them up and stands by their side. Sometimes the other half is part of their household, and sometimes they are a sibling or lifelong friend. Once in awhile, they are simply two people who connected at a time and place in their lives when they needed each other.

The partner relationship is fascinating. The relationship is symbiotic and deep. It is one that many people never discover unless they are willing to truly love. Loving, sharing, and connecting involve as much risk as they involve pure joy. These relationships create a sense of truly living and offering yourself to the service of another human being. As my dad and Phil and Audrey taught me, this is one of the greatest gifts of all—service to another human being.

There are people who, no matter what life hands them, carry dignity, compassion, and joy in their hearts. They have a peace that separates them because they have been through more than most. In the end, they have come to find out that they do not have to be in control. "Trust me, child, I have it all under control. Love, God" is a sign that I keep in my house. It reminds me that when life is tough, it is not up to me to fight it but to embrace what I have to learn from it and to carry on with my head high and my heart open. This is what I see in my clients. This is what I saw in my dad. They know they are not being "buried." They are where they are in order to grow, to evolve, to live this one, wild, precious life we are all given to its fullest. In fact, maybe it is quite the opposite: they carry the gift because they found out early on that the weight of the world does not rest on them. It seems the sooner we discover that, the happier we become.

We All Start as Strangers

When I first started training, I worked out of my garage. Many of my early clients from my "garage days" stayed with me or stayed connected across the miles. Why? How did I get so lucky? What is it that makes them come back?

Together, we discovered exercise as an outlet to reduce stress and claim an hour of time for ourselves. What keeps us close now is empathy and understanding. We have looked each other in the eye again and again. We have aged together and been through a period in our lives where we are okay in our own skin. The goal of looking a certain way has been replaced with the goal of good health. The things we thought we were looking for are not as important as they once seemed. They never were. Bina, one of my "garage days" clients, narrowed it down like this, "All things we are seeking are nothing compared to what we already possess. We are thankful for the skin we are in."

Yes, we are.

Why? Because it holds our gift to the world. And more than that, it signifies that we are each right where we are meant to be. The quote attributed to Plato, "Be kind. Everyone you meet is fighting a hard battle," is my guide when I am with my clients, and I am inspired by the words of Pope Francis, "Heal the wounds, heal the wounds . . . And you have to start from the ground up."

When I see the beauty and the strength radiate from the inside of my clients—young, old, covered in scars, sparked by curiosity, naïve with youth, bursting with possibility, and even those hiding in ego and insecurities—I am overwhelmed with love. They have the courage to share their hearts so that I can see what is on the inside and the willingness to connect meaningfully. Through our interactions, our stories become one and create the context for generations to come.

Isn't it the most wonderful compensation in life that we all start as strangers and leave as friends? That is a life well lived. To leave those whose lives we touched better is one of the greatest gifts of life. During my "garage days," when I did not know my future and was unaware of my potential, I was surrounded by these beautiful people. It reminds me of the words in the title of a poem by Jon York, "Keep the ones who heard you when you never said a word." Their trust in me is humbling, and I am beyond grateful to have them by my side, then, now, and, if we are so lucky, tomorrow. I am also thankful for their authenticity. They are my tribe, my heartbeat, my people who exemplify "real." Our relationship has withstood the test of time, and we know that "the skin we are in" is just right.

My dad did not get to live as long as Phil and Audrey and many of my other clients. Will I live a long life? Will you live a long life? Does it even matter if we are living confident, happy, and in love with "the skin we are in"?

Thank you for letting me be a part of your story. As you read this chapter, we connected and are no longer strangers. Your story has become mine, and mine, yours. I hope the effect we have had on each other is mutual. I challenge you to continue to connect, to serve, and to love. Love hard. Care deeply. Share your stories. Use your love to reach out and help others. Weave these threads of life together, and you will live a purposeful, meaningful, and incredibly strong life.

ACTION STEP

What's your story?

Knowing your own story and being able to put it into words go a long way toward helping you connect with others.

Take some time to write out your story or record it in some way.

Then share your story with someone else.

Sharing our experiences with others helps us to better serve and love each other. Together, we create a strong life.

About Jill Ruth Rooks

I am a New Jersey girl living in a Southern California world with my husband and teenage son and daughter. My passion is health and how our mindset affects physical fitness.

In 2011, I created The Energy Lab in Redlands, CA. It is a family business that my husband and I work in every day. We see hundreds of beautifully authentic and diverse people come through our doors, seeking fitness, health and wellness. Most come to work out and exercise their bodies. All leave with their energies shifted, spirits lifted, and smiles on their faces.

Our fitness studio focuses on play, variability, and longevity. I focus on educating our team of coaches with resources to serve our community. With certifications from cycling to T'ai Chi and TRX to Jungshin I love to learn all I can about the human body. I have spent the last two decades studying and teaching what makes people tick. I listen and guide people along paths of wellness for long-term health solutions and overall ease of living.

I have been asked to present for organizations ranging from Rotary Clubs to local running groups to Loma Linda University Health Women's Conference. I co-hosted the health and fitness segment of

About Redlands Radio on ABC's KMET 1490AM, and I guest lecture for the Loma Linda School of Allied Health Physical Therapy Program.

I love teaching corrective exercise, and I am blessed to work with special populations including cerebral palsy and multiple sclerosis, along with stroke victims, cancer survivors, and people with Alzheimer's.

I am not yet my finished product.

My association with the Todd Durkin Mastermind Platinum Level and with my Institute of Motion Level 3 peers and coaches fuels, challenges, and supports me. Fascial dissection courses with Thomas Myers have revealed the world under the skin and taught me humility and love for the beauty of life.

Jill Ruth Rooks

The Energy Lab

www.energylabfitness.com

Instagram: @the_energy_lab

Facebook: @energylabfitness

CHAPTER 2

Believe in Yourself

by Tim Rhode

If there is one thing that leads to **strong living**, it is believing in yourself. It is the starting point for all progress, persistence, and achievement. It drives what you will or will not do, and how you will or will not go about it. What you believe about yourself can be liberating, limiting, or both. Optimism, determination, and resilience are all extensions of what you believe. Unfortunately, so are pessimism, reluctance, and hesitation.

If you have ever found yourself trapped between inspiration and inaction, or living with unfulfilled dreams and aspirations, my hope is that the next few pages will help you to understand both why and how you can **believe in yourself** to reach greater heights of success and fulfillment.

What Does It Mean to "Believe in Yourself"?

Is it self-confidence?

The dictionary defines self-confidence as a general self-assurance with your judgment and ability to engage successfully in life overall; or, a belief in your ability to succeed in specific situations or accomplish specific tasks. It is essentially what you think or feel you are capable of doing.

For example, you might have an overall sense of confidence but doubt your ability to succeed with specific tasks, like starting a business or writing a book. Or, you may be quite confident that you can drive your car safely (a specific and important task) but lack the general confidence necessary to step out of your comfort zone to try new things or grow as a person. Understanding the limitations we place on ourselves based on the stories we have created about our lives is vital to self-awareness and understanding.

Is it self-esteem?

Self-confidence is not the same as self-esteem. Self-confidence is believing in what you can do. Self-esteem is what you believe about your own worth—liking yourself for what you are capable of and what you have done. From my perspective, believing in yourself involves all three of these—general self-confidence, confidence in your ability to tackle specific challenges, and your sense of self-worth.

Where Does This Come From?

You certainly develop confidence from trying things and succeeding. You balance the bike. You catch the ball. Your date says yes when you ask her out for dinner. It is easy to believe in yourself when you try things that work out.

But what if they don't? Are you doomed then to never achieve confidence? Or worse—lose any confidence you previously had?

Certainly not.

Look at Thomas Edison, who tried and failed more than 10,000 times before he developed a working electric light bulb. Or consider Colonel Sanders, who pitched his chicken recipe to more than 60 prospects before he experienced success. In fact, their belief in themselves and their ability to succeed very likely kept them in the game until they prevailed. So where did they get their belief? And can you get yours the same way?

I believe you can.

Believing in yourself is a choice!

Have you ever believed something in spite of the immediate evidence that it is risky or unlikely to work?

Of course, many people do.

What we believe is a choice—not a consequence.

It is a choice that you can make (or un-make) at any time. I have seen it over and over, and experienced it myself on many occasions.

When I first went to high school, I was not very big. I weighed less than 100 pounds until halfway through my freshman year, but I thought it would be fun to play football. (I was not very smart either!) I wanted to try out for the team, but the coach pulled me aside and told me I was too small. He would not even let my try out. I was crushed. I tried to convince him that you couldn't tackle what you couldn't catch, but he was having none of it.

Instead, I chose to run for student office (class president). As an incoming freshman from a smaller school, I was not well known and was beaten badly by a popular kid whom everyone seemed to know and like. Talk about a blow to my self-esteem—this was a double whammy!

Rather than give up, I decided to focus on what I could learn and contribute. I focused on what I had to give, rather than on what I was not getting. This turned out to be a useful approach to life.

I got involved with the student council. There were no size limits or elections there. If you showed up, you were in. I spoke up, served on committees, organized fundraisers, and worked as a liaison between our class, the faculty, and administration. I had fun, learned a ton, and got to know many more people.

Sophomore year, I ran again for class president—and this time I won. And I won again in my junior year. Our class was doing well and excelling in inter-class competitions.

Senior year, I chose not to run. I was humbled to learn that some of my classmates decided for me that they were putting my name on the ballot. They did, and I was elected. This was the most satisfying win I had experienced in my life thus far. I did not ask for it, I did not go after it. It was given to me based on others' belief in my self-confidence. I was rewarded for giving back to others. It was one of the proudest moments of my late childhood.

The lessons I learned and experience gained from that involvement served me well over the years. Perhaps the most important lesson was choosing to believe in myself and in what I had to contribute, in spite of a few defeats. I stayed in the game by finding the best position for me to play.

It is a choice. No one else can make the choice for you, and you cannot make it for anyone else. It is all up to you!

Angela Duckworth, in her wonderful book, *Grit: The Power and Passion of Perseverance*, cites the Chinese saying, "Down 7, up 8." That idea is echoed by H.G. Wells, who said, "If you fell down yesterday, stand up today." Both pearls of wisdom encourage us to believe—to make that choice—even if it is for the 8th time.

Here is my point:

> *Anything in life that you do, attempt, or even consider will turn out better if you believe in yourself than if you don't.*

What Will Believing in Yourself Do for You?

If you could choose, which life would you rather live—one filled with hesitation, trepidation, uncertainty, reluctance, and obscurity, or one that is definite, intentional, confident, remarkable, and influential?

We, likely, all do some of both. It is not an either-or proposition.

So, let me ask the question in another way: which approach do you use most often? And are you improving?

It is a choice. That choice is determined by whether, and the extent to which, you believe in yourself.

Let's look at leadership.

The first requirement of leadership is that people are willing to follow. If you envision yourself as a leader, a change agent, or a difference-maker, know this: **people follow confidence**.

Think about it. The people we follow and admire—the leaders, authors, actors, athletes—are all brimming with confidence. It matters less how you look or what your background is than the extent to which you believe in yourself and the conviction you exhibit.

I have seen many unlikely people with bestselling books and a history of success serving as keynote speakers, commanding a stage in front of thousands who are hanging on their every word. I have seen other people in sports or business rise from obscurity to greatness, bypassing those who were smarter, more talented, taller, stronger, and faster, mainly because **they believed in themselves** and did what it took to succeed.

People follow confidence.
If you believe in yourself, others will too.

What If You Lack Confidence?

Not believing in yourself means you doubt your ability to do something. This often shows itself in the form of hesitation, delay, or procrastination. Hesitation is sometimes good, especially if it keeps us from making a foolish decision or doing something we would regret later. I prefer to view this as contemplation rather than hesitation. But if you find yourself hesitating, ask yourself, "Why?" Then get the information or help you need, and make the choice. Most great leaders have been recognized not because of what they already knew, but rather, because of their beliefs, the choices they made, and the confidence they then exhibited and inspired in others.

What If You Are Uncertain?

A lack of confidence should not be confused with uncertainty. Even those with confidence and conviction face uncertainty. The difference is that confident people do not get stuck on it. Uncertainty just means that a choice is necessary. Even if the uncertainty is about your ability to do something, you still need to make the choice. Will you try it or not? Will you take action or not? You may have to get information or help to make the choice, but do not allow what you are unsure about to morph into perpetual avoidance or procrastination.

Here is an important point:

*Not knowing the way should not be
confused with unwilling to begin.*

Uncertainty need not erode confidence. The Wright brothers, Lindberg, Edison, Einstein, Durkin, Jobs, all had uncertainties, but history has proven that they believed enough in their ability to figure things out. They had to believe in themselves, even through great uncertainty, in order to persevere, to prevail, and to achieve.

Some refer to this as the "tyranny of how." The "how" can be figured out. You have to start with the "why" and "what" you want in life, then you figure out the "how." But do not let the "how" stop you. Those who succeed keep going. You can, too.

What If You REALLY Lack Confidence?

Persistent lack of confidence can grow to insecurity. A big challenge with insecurity is that it is often less visible. Perhaps even a blind spot. Who knows what insecurities our friends and colleagues harbor? Often, the best way to learn people's insecurities is to watch for what they are NOT doing. This is especially important in the workplace. Have you ever hired or worked with someone who consistently failed to do an important part of their job? Chances are that some level of insecurity is at the heart of the problem. If they believed enough in themselves and their ability to succeed, that part of the job would be done—perhaps even with exceptional results.

Fortunately, lack of confidence and insecurities can be turned around. We are definitely not stuck with them forever. As a friend, leader, or supporter, you can ask questions and try to help yourself or others find their source of insecurity. What are other people dealing with? Perhaps it is not workplace-related. It could be family, kids, past experiences, or something else. Getting to the bottom of it and recognizing the effect it is having is the first step in overcoming. Follow that with encouragement and action steps or baby steps that build confidence, and you will be helping yourself or others to overcome insecurities and invisible roadblocks. Once we accomplish something, it is with us forever. Think about riding a bike—from impossible balancing act to lifelong skill set. It is forever.

The Price of Insecurity

Insecurity or not believing in ourselves sufficiently to act on our inspirations may be the single biggest expense in our society today. What price are you paying for your unfulfilled dreams and visions? I am not just talking about the unrealized economics, but also the emotional expense of not achieving what is in your heart.

Joel Osteen, author, evangelist, and pastor of Lakewood Church in Houston, Texas, explained, "The wealthiest neighborhoods in America are the cemeteries, where people have been buried with their brilliant but unfulfilled ideas for businesses, inventions, wisdom, books, and movies." He was referring to the untold genius and inspiration that was never shared because those people did not believe enough in their ability to make their dreams happen. They literally DID take it with them. Willingness to take action, to take the first or the next step was the ONLY thing standing in their way.

Do not go to your grave with your dreams and aspirations unfulfilled; at least fully commit to and attempt them with all you have in your heart. Do not waste another moment. Believe in yourself enough to get started, to make good choices, to overcome challenges, and to succeed. The price of insecurity is regret, and it is too high of a price to pay.

The biggest challenge we will ever face is ourselves._

How Can You Create More Belief in Yourself?

"Do I first have to try and succeed?" is a question many of us contemplate. Succeeding with anything is certain to boost self-confidence, but I do not believe you must first prove your capabilities in order to believe in yourself. This is precisely the approach that keeps people stuck in mediocrity.

Confidence and success are like the chicken and the egg. Which comes first? Success can certainly lead to confidence, but confidence will also lead to success. My view? Success comes at the end of something. Confidence is available to you now, and confidence paves the way to success.

It is a choice. You can DO this. Why not start with what is available now?

Another common question, "Should I fake it 'til I make it?" We have all heard this cliché and perhaps even used it with some success. I am not a fan of false bravado. It is easy to see and even easier to see through. Deciding to believe in yourself, even with a lack of experience or success, can be genuine. It does not have to be fake or false.

"Should I wear rose-colored glasses?" Life is not all rainbows and unicorns. It pays to anticipate potential problems. I know many people who have a healthy respect for Murphy's Law: if anything can go wrong, it will. However, they proceed in pursuit of their goals and dreams. Forewarned is forearmed. But I know many who put more faith in

Murphy than they do in themselves. They are so sure something will go wrong that they never even try.

Here is a proven method to proceed: remember that believing in yourself is a choice—one you can make consciously and repeatedly until it is no longer necessary to remind yourself. I began this at an early age and still do it—especially when facing a challenge or following a loss.

It was 1968 and the summer before fifth grade. I was 10 years old and visiting my cousins in Illinois. I knew my mother was very ill. I had heard people calling it "cancer." All of a sudden one night, my sister and I were whisked up in blankets and pajamas to make a high-speed trip home to Wisconsin where my mom was in the hospital. We arrived in time to give her a kiss, and then she was gone.

Even though we were surrounded by people offering consolation and support, I felt so alone. She was my rock. She was my biggest fan. She was the one who had convinced me that I could do anything in life that I put my mind to.

It took a few days, but I knew that I had a choice to make—give up and go to pieces, or believe in myself and prove her right. I chose to believe in myself.

The next years were tough. My dad remarried. We moved away— new town, new family, new school, new friends. There were plenty of challenges, for sure. But it was the crucible that tested and developed my confidence and resolve.

More than once in my life I have had to begin again. Rather than withdraw, each time I have chosen to learn and grow. Each time I regained or exceeded my prior accomplishments and gained valuable experience and perspective.

Whether you think you can or you can't, you're right.
—Henry Ford

Building Your Belief—Affirmation

You are a valuable resource to any team and any effort with which you become involved. Read that sentence again (and again), and you will be on to one of the best ways to improve your beliefs. Affirmations are simply inspiring lines that remind us to be and do our best.

The Food and Drug Administration should add a recommended daily allowance (RDA) of affirmation to their requirements for a healthy diet and lifestyle. This is real "vitamin A." Imagine a world where everyone begins their day reminding themselves of their value, potential, and best intentions to reinforce a productive, positive self-image. How long would it take for things to move in a positive direction?

There are many great sources of helpful affirmations these days. With a few minutes and an Internet connection, you can be on your way to an increasingly firm foundation of solid beliefs (I'll give you some of my favorite sources at the end of this chapter). There are even apps that will send them to you at the start of every day.

Pick affirmations that resonate with you and how you envision your best life.

Too many great options for affirmations? Keep it fresh and rotate new ones every month. Put them where you can access them easily or even post them visibly—the bathroom mirror is a favorite location. Recite them at least once per day, preferably out loud. Before you know it, your confidence will begin showing the way. People will be attracted to you because you believe in yourself.

While we are on the subject of affirmations, some of the most effective ones are those you write yourself, tailored to your specific needs. Here is one I wrote more than twenty years ago. I found myself in a dead-end role, managing a business and having to implement the will and whims of people with whom I did not agree. I needed the work but was frustrated that I was wasting my time, life, and talent. Rather than remain stuck, I directed my frustration to pen and paper, and crafted my vision and intentions. This has inspired me time and again.

A MEANINGFUL PART OF THE SUM

You are in charge

Of your life

And your daily activities which will add up to be your life.

You will decide

to act or to react,

to be positive or negative.

Act positively in all situations.

You are the master

Of your attitude

Your attention, your priorities,

And ultimately, your destiny.

You will determine

The pace

And the order

With which your life is lived

Take this day and make it

a meaningful part of the sum.

It was not long before I went from being stuck, to helping people and businesses on three continents. My work began to be published frequently in national and global trade journals, and we launched a business that offered a new way to achieve wellness. That business employed and trained hundreds of fitness professionals, helped tens of thousands of people to live longer and live stronger, and generated more than $170M in revenue over the next 20 years.

While there are other affirmations I have come to rely upon, this one remains alongside my bathroom sink, albeit a bit tattered and worn, where I read it nearly every morning. It has withstood the test of time and continues to bolster a belief in my ability and determination to make every day count.

The Value of Conviction—Can You Believe in Yourself Too Much?

Perhaps. Excessive self-confidence can be unbecoming. It often appears as bluster, false bravado, or arrogance—none of which are attractive or helpful. But that is not the biggest problem.

While those traits are certainly undesirable and may not be socially redeeming, far more often the problem is not too much, but rather too little confidence. For every person who thinks too highly of themselves, there are dozens, if not hundreds more, hindered to some degree by their limiting self-beliefs.

More is better than less, and a lot is better than more. In fact, an abundance of self-confidence becomes conviction. **It is with conviction that success is most commonly found in any endeavor.**

Conviction is a fixed or firm belief. If that belief is in yourself, in your ability to navigate the waters and challenges of your life, then you will be far more certain to meet with success. This is the message of my all-time favorite quote by Henry David Thoreau:

"If one advances confidently in the direction of his dreams and endeavors to live the life which he has imagined, he will meet with a success unexpected in common hours."

Conviction is the way of the achievers. I have seen this time and again as I have worked with athletes, trainers, salespeople, managers, and leaders. I spent much of the past year working with more than 200 personal trainers, helping them grow their businesses and personal incomes. It was quite apparent that the uncertain struggle, the confident succeed, and those with conviction thrive.

The difference between confidence and conviction is the difference between good and great. People with confidence are solid and reliable. They show up, and they get the job done. That is all good. But those with conviction lead. They lead their teams. They lead their industries. They lead in income. And most often, they lead the way for others to succeed.

Confidence or conviction? It is your choice.

You Can Help!

Believing in yourself can be infectious! A person with a great deal of self-confidence can get others to do good things they would not otherwise have considered. There is no better example of this than Todd Durkin who wrote the foreword to this book. Todd is a mentor to hundreds of fitness professionals, and he is an inspiration to millions with his prolific insight and encouragement. He is brimming with confidence and inspires confidence in others. We can all follow his example:

Believe in Yourself. Live a Strong Life. Spread It to Others.

This can be your gift to the world.

Believe in yourself! If you do, so will everyone else!

---

*Affirmation resources that I recommend:

Here's one from Ray Davis, Founder of The Affirmation Spot,

And another at FreeAffirmations.org

Enjoy!

ACTION STEPS

1. Read the classic book, *Think and Grow Rich,* by Napoleon Hill

After meeting and studying the most successful people of his time, Hill realized that "Whatever the mind of man can believe, it can achieve."

I first read this great book at age 26. I began to believe, no matter how unlikely, that if I thought, dreamed, or imagined something, I must have the ability (somehow) to make it happen. This changed my life forever.

"Whatever the mind of man can believe, it can achieve."
—Napoleon Hill

2. Assemble or create your affirmations.

Go to the affirmations sites mentioned below and find the ones that speak to you. Better yet, take some time to write your own. Put them where you can see and read them every day. Say them out loud, if possible, and let them soak into your soul. Let your beliefs carry you like a winner.

3. Start now

Ask what you've really been wanting to do but have been putting off. Make a list, if necessary. Pick one. Know that if you've thought of it that you can achieve it. Write down the things you need to do and get started. (This is one of those times where believing in yourself leads to success.) Continue to accomplish the items on your list until your goal is achieved. Success will not only improve your confidence with specific tasks, but also your overall confidence as an achiever, along with your self-esteem.

4. Spread the word

If this chapter moved you, share it with others. Or just make it part of who you are to help others to believe in themselves. Imagine a world where everyone believed in themselves and their ability to succeed. Let's start now - with you and the people you know.

5. Share your success

Join our community! Go to the Strong Living Facebook Group at https:// www.facebook.com/groups/117534395460999/. Share your affirmations and your success. Tell us about your goals, actions and achievements as a result of reading this book. #BelieveInYou

ABOUT TIM RHODE

With 30+ years of experience in the health, fitness, and recreation industries, Tim Rhode is co-founder of the Maryland Athletic Club & Wellness Center (MAC) in Baltimore, MD, and president of Rhode Management Company. He has successfully managed multipurpose athletic clubs up to 120,000 square feet with more than 300 employees.

Tim served as president of the Mid-Atlantic Club Management Association (MACMA) and also as a member of the International Health Racquet and Sportsclub Association (IHRSA) Board of Directors, and chaired the Fitness Industry Strategic Planning Committee.

Tim consulted for health and wellness facilities in England, Australia, and throughout the United States. He has been a certified ACE presenter and speaker at leading industry conferences on the subjects of management, marketing, sales management, team building, employee accountability, performance compensation, strategic planning, and success motivation.

In addition to his work in the health club industry, in 2009, Tim was a founding director of the Coalition for a Healthy Maryland, a community organization working to promote health improvement and disease prevention in the state, and to deter the state legislature from approving the governor's proposal to tax health club dues. For four consecutive years CFAHM was successful at defeating the tax initiative and in the process initiated Healthy Maryland Day and then Healthy Maryland Week, both of which drew statewide publicity. He also served a 3-year term on the board of trustees of the Maryland chapter of the National Multiple Sclerosis Society.

Tim and his wife, Liz, have two children: T.J., age 19, and Jake, 13.

Tim Rhode

Rhode Management Company

http://rhodemanagement.com

Facebook: @timrhode

CHAPTER 3

RISE UP!

by Preston Smith

***Our greatest glory is not in never falling
but in rising every time we fall.***
— Confucius

Have you ever made a mistake? I mean, a BIG mistake? A mistake so big, in fact, that it completely destroyed a dream that you worked long and hard to achieve? You completely sabotaged your dream by making one poor decision, and suddenly your dream was no longer within reach—have you ever done anything like that?

I have.

It was the winter of 1989 in the Shenandoah Valley—Staunton, VA, to be exact. Staunton is a small town, mostly admired for its historic downtown shopping and impeccable preservation of its rich history and scenic views. *Southern Living* magazine called it one of the prettiest and most progressive towns in the South, and while I couldn't agree more with the magazine's description of my hometown, I, along with many other Virginians, recognize Staunton as a basketball powerhouse.

The "Leemen" of Robert E. Lee High School in Staunton, VA, have won seven state championships to date. Head Coach Paul Hatcher is the winningest coach in state history, and in 1989 I was the starting forward on what would become Hatcher's fourth state championship team. On this particular day, in practice, I was not feeling like one of the five best players on the team. Coach asked me to change jerseys and play on the B team, second string. We were going to scrimmage the A team, the starters. I always felt like the coach had it out for me, and that day was no different. It infuriated me to play on the B team, but it made me play really, really hard.

I played center on the B team because I was the tallest player, and I refused to let the A team's center, Reggie Waddy, back down anyone else in the paint but me. He was the most athletic player on the team, and he'd nearly dunked on me in the play before. I was not about to let it happen again. Fortunately, I was pressing against Waddy's back so hard that he received the ball in poor position and passed it out to the perimeter to Marcus Reed. Marcus Reed would eventually go on to replace me permanently on the A team. He was a talented underclassman who handled the ball well and played with a lot of heart.

Out of nowhere the whistle blew, and Coach Hatcher walked onto the floor. He instructed us to line up on the baseline for some end-of-practice conditioning. We usually did sprints to close out practice, and that day was no different. My heart was set on being the first to complete the sprints since I'd suffered defeat to the A team two times already that day. I won the sprints, but I just could not seem to win the affection of my coach who seemed to do things just to get me angry. In hindsight, though, putting me on the B team was nothing compared to what he would do next.

That day, after practice, a teammate asked me to give him a ride to a mall about twenty miles or so from Staunton to purchase a new pair of shoes. He said he had stolen a credit card the night before, and he wanted to try to use it before the owner noticed it was missing. Since I was always desperate for a pair of shoes and was one of only three guys on the team who had a car, I agreed to the terms that I would take him if he got me a pair too. We agreed, and against my better judgment, I gave him a ride to the mall. Little did I know that the only thing this deal would bring was an end to my basketball career.

I drove north on Interstate 81 without giving much thought to what I was about to do. In my mind, nothing could go wrong for me because all I had to do was provide the transportation. My friend was doing the real dirty work.

We entered the store at different times and parted ways. Shortly after my soon-to-be accomplice approached the counter, I could tell our scheme was not going as planned. Before I knew it, someone was announcing a cryptic code over the loudspeaker. The jig was up.

Somewhere, someone was being alerted to the fact that my friend did not own this credit card.

We quickly left the store without any interference from security or police, and thankfully we were not arrested and sent to jail.

On the way home, I seemed to be even more nervous than I was on the way to Valley Mall. Something just didn't sit right with me. I just kept having eerie feelings. Were cameras in the store? Did anyone take a picture of us? Or my license plates? Were the police going to suddenly pull me over? Nothing of the sort happened, and by the time we made it home, I thought we might be in the clear.

44

The following Monday afternoon, just two days after the mall incident, I was called to the school office by Principal Hamilton. I could not help but wonder if this had anything to do with Friday evening, but as nervous as I was, I kept thinking there was no way that news could travel so quickly. This visit had to be regarding a different matter.

When I entered the principal's office, I saw my teammate and soon-to-be co-defendant. I sat down, and the principal began by telling us that he was contacted by the Harrisonburg Police Department regarding the attempted use of a stolen credit card. I could not believe my ears. How did they find us so quickly? Where did we go wrong? And how was this going to impact my life?

I was in BIG trouble, and I knew there was no way out of it. It did not feel good or look good for me. This was not my typical behavior, and all I could think about was how disappointed my parents were going to be. What was I going to say to them? How were they going to react? Was Coach going to find out? And, if so, what was his reaction going to be?

I had been in the basketball system since the eighth grade and remember players being removed or kicked off the team, but I NEVER thought, in a million years, it would happen to me. I had never broken the law before in my life, and my grades were good. I had never even considered that this kind of punishment would come my way.

Perhaps that is why I believed there was a glimmer of hope that somehow, some way, I would be able to stay on the team despite my poor decision. Would my longstanding relationship with my coach get me pardoned? I had been a part of the Lee High School basketball system ever since I was eligible to play, and surely Coach knew how much I loved this game. Maybe the fact that I was now a three-year varsity player who was interested in becoming a student-athlete on the collegiate level would be my saving grace or that we lived in the same neighborhood or that his son and I were friends or that I was an honor roll student. And on and on and on. I was hoping for a miracle, but I knew how stern Coach could be.

That Monday, at practice, Coach pulled me to the side and told me not to get dressed. He was suspending me, indefinitely, until more information was brought forth regarding the mall incident on Friday. Talk about swift justice. In less than 72 hours my crime had come to light, and my career was in jeopardy. News travels fast, and bad news travels even faster.

Within a couple of weeks, indefinite suspension turned into full removal, and my basketball career ended abruptly. It was a career which began at six years old at the YMCA less than a mile from my house and went on to include thousands of hours practicing and playing. I take full responsibility for my actions, and I believe I should have been held accountable. But being permanently removed from the team was too harsh of a punishment. If only I could have hung in there for the last 27 games of my career, I would have had the chance to see if, and where, I could have played college basketball. I think my chances would have been good considering my team won the State AA Championship with a perfect 32–0 record, and every starting player went on to play on the collegiate level.

Initially, I believed that not going on to play collegiate basketball was the biggest loss that came from being removed from my high school varsity basketball team. But, I finally figured out that the biggest loss was the two decades it took me to find a new passion.

I will be the first to admit that my journey to finding a new passion probably took longer than necessary. The early end to my basketball career hurt me tremendously, and I was in a slump for a long time. I thought the world had come to an end. But the truth is, my life was far from over, which brings me to one of the key lessons learned from my high school basketball experience. According to Tony Robbins, "You never actually fail, you just don't get the outcome you expected." And my basketball experience is proof of this.

Thankfully, I had positive people around me who reminded me of Tony Robbins' wisdom and helped me put things into perspective. I realized that I had to stop playing the victim role and release the chains from that devastating experience that were holding me back. I had to shift my thinking from negative to positive. What lessons did I learn? How could I take my foundational skills from basketball and apply them to something else that would bring me the same amount of joy? The turning point came as soon as I shifted my thinking. I was able to see new and exciting possibilities. I had something to work towards. I was inspired, and that gave me the fuel I needed to rise up.

Today I am a personal trainer, and the fire is back. I feel like I am, once again, living a strong life that excites me daily. I have my own business where I use things I learned from my basketball days. That experience helped me develop and flourish in my career much faster than I would have otherwise. At the heart of basketball lies human movement and lots of strength training and conditioning. Both were embedded in me at a very early age.

Aside from the personal lessons I learned through my basketball experience are the lessons I learned about coaching. As a personal trainer, it is my responsibility to coach from the heart. It is more than helping someone lose weight, train for a marathon, or rehabilitate a knee. I also see the value of making a personal connection with my clients and helping them transform completely—mind, body, and spirit. If one of my clients gets off-track or does something out of the norm, I will not dismiss them completely from achieving their goals as my coach did. I believe in taking time to understand, motivate, and inspire others to see the vision and help them stay the course to be the best they can be. This lesson helped me to positively impact lives in a way that I never imagined.

I know, for sure, that my life as a heart-centered personal trainer is the life I was destined to live. What I once thought of as the worst mistake of my life turned out to be an opportunity to rise up and accept the greater purpose in store for me. Due to my experience with basketball and the mistakes I made, both on and off the court, I came into the fitness industry with an understanding of how to fully use my passion for sports and strength training to improve the lives of others. I turned my mistake into a triumph. And you can too.

Your story may look different than mine. But we all make mistakes or have minor setbacks at some point in our lives. Whether you have a constant struggle with meeting your fitness goals or you have made a mistake that impacted your career or personal life, do not sit around stuck in failure mode. Do not let your setbacks define you. Learn from them and move on.

Author Craig Ballantyne said it best: "The mistakes of your past have taught you the lessons you need to create the solutions for your life." That's exactly what happened to me, and you can make it happen for you too—find the lessons. Stay open to new possibilities. Be positive, and rise up!

ACTION STEP

Think about a moment in your life when you made a mistake. What did you do? How do you view that mistake? Did it help you or hurt you?

Make a list of all the ways that the mistake helped you. What did your choices do FOR you? How did your choices help you in your life? What positive things have happened in your life because you made that mistake? What lessons have you learned?

Taking a few moments to recognize that mistakes are opportunities is how you, too, will rise up to live your strongest life.

About Preston Smith

Preston Smith is a certified personal trainer through the National Academy of Sports Medicine. A sports and fitness enthusiast from Virginia, he received his BS in criminal justice from Virginia Commonwealth University. After spending time in sales, he left the field to pursue his true passion of fitness. He started out in a "big box" gym and is now the owner of Preston Ray Fitness.

Since becoming a personal trainer, Preston has acquired five additional certifications: Performance Enhancement Specialist, Corrective Exercise Specialist, Precision Nutrition Specialist, TRX, and Animal Flow. Personal training allows him to share his love of sports and knowledge of exercise science in a purposeful manner.

Preston credits the Todd Durkin Mastermind Group with helping him find his way in the fitness industry. He is a Platinum member and works with a team of more than 150 of the country's top fitness professionals. Together they strategize daily on everything from personal development to opening your own gym. The group gathers bi-annually to develop their skills face-to-face.

He is also a member of John Spencer Ellis' Penthouse Group that is devoted to improving members' lifestyles and finances. Preston loves to learn and make new friends.

Preston's philosophy on training is to have the mind of a beginner: "You don't have to be an expert to look and feel better. You just have to have a beginner's mind. In the beginner's mind, there are so many possibilities. In the expert's mind, there are few."

When Preston is not at the gym, he is perfecting his fitness craft by reading, laughing, and spending time with his wife and two children.

Preston Smith, CSCS

Owner, Preston Ray Fitness

http://www.prestonrayfitness.com

Instagram: @prestonrayfitness

Facebook: @PrestonRaySmith

CHAPTER 4

FIND YOUR VOICE

by Amanda Mittleman

There is a busy coffee shop two blocks from UCLA Medical Center. It sits right next door to one of the original Fox Studio movie theaters. For several months, I spent five to six hours a week sitting in that coffee shop, people-watching, thinking, and writing. Somewhere in the middle of those hours, I walked over to my thirty-minute vocal therapy appointment at the UCLA Medical Center and then returned to the busy little coffee shop to resume my writing. California rush hour traffic created this opportunity for me. There was a time when I would not have viewed this as an "opportunity." There was a time when I dreamed of having the time to be able to write. As it turns out, obstacles can become opportunities with the right mindset.

Before My Surgery

The first time I saw my otolaryngologist at UCLA I was annoyed and in a hurry to get in and out of my appointment as quickly as possible. I own Mo-Mentum Fitness, a fitness and wellness studio in Huntington Beach, California. I teach two to three group fitness classes, train five to fifteen people in small group or personal training sessions, and lead a team of twelve trainers and membership services professionals every day. Then, I attempt to be the best wife and mother of four I can possibly be. It will not surprise you that the superhero I relate to most is Wonder Woman. In reality, my time is limited, so the thought of sitting in Southern California traffic in the middle of the day frustrated me.

My mission for more than twenty years has been to help people unlock their innate potentials to live extraordinary lives by overcoming their own perceived limitations. This passion began at the age of 21 when I became a single mother of twins who were born twelve weeks prematurely. The birth of my twins, becoming a single mother, and the necessity to advocate for my babies in a complex medical system introduced me to the lioness that had been hiding dormant inside of me.

When my babies were two years old and further away from the dangers of prematurity, I went back to college. Shortly after that, I started teaching aerobics and personal training at a local gym because I could not afford a gym membership and childcare. It was that job, helping people become stronger inside and out, that became my calling. Fitness became my tool to help people find and unlock their dormant strengths, just like the people along my path had helped me uncover mine.

My twins amazed their doctors and continued to get stronger and healthier every year. I graduated from college with a master's degree, married an incredible man, and inherited two beautiful stepchildren. We became a family of six. My life was filled with love. When my kids were all in high school, I opened Mo-Mentum Fitness. The trials in my life helped me become a driven, passionate, and strong woman. I thought I was living a strong life.

But that day, while I waited for my otolaryngologist, a nagging feeling of suspense sat in my belly like a rock. My mind tried to figure out how I'd ended up in this doctor's office. I was supposed to be the example of health. For years, I had preached that we get only one body to live in while we are on this earth, and by choosing daily actions to keep that body strong and healthy, we can live extraordinary lives. I taught everyone I worked with that the strongest lives were lived with courage and hard work, by making time to recover and play and by surrounding ourselves with the people we loved.

Sitting in that quiet doctor's office, I realized that I had drifted off course. I was definitely working hard. I loved my work, and I was working towards my vision and my mission every day. But I was fighting to make time for my family. I had slowly drifted away from playing and recovering at all. If I was honest with myself, my mind and body were exhausted all of the time, and I was ignoring the warning signs.

As a result of those long hours of training, teaching, and coaching, my voice had become increasingly raspy. Over a period of two years, it took more and more energy to push air through my vocal cords at enough velocity to produce a voice. Some days my voice worked, and some days, no matter how hard I pushed, it simply would not work. Almost daily for those two years, people who did not know me assumed I was sick with laryngitis and would tell me they hoped I felt better soon. It was a nice gesture, but my heart sank every time I heard these words. I did not have laryngitis. I was not sick. My vocal cords were failing me.

I worked hard to ignore this problem, hoping it would just disappear. My raspy voice was becoming inaudible and had begun to interfere with my relationships and my mission. I pushed my vocal cords super hard even when I could feel the swelling in my throat. Instead of being concerned, I was frustrated. To be honest, it was my friends who actually bullied me into making this appointment and driving all the way to UCLA to see this highly recommended otolaryngologist and head and neck surgeon.

54

I only followed through because my body was tired and even my hardest pushing did not work anymore.

My first appointment only took about 15 minutes (followed by two more hours driving home.) The doctor looked in my throat with his magic microscope wand, and there it was, a very large bump called a polyp sitting on my right vocal cord. A female vocal cord is about 1.25 centimeters in length, so in vocal cord units, my giant polyp was about one quarter of a centimeter long. My doctor told me the surgery would be quick, followed by one week of complete vocal rest and three more weeks of limited talking. I was not happy with this inconvenient option, but it sounded doable. I let my "bully" friends know that they were right and headed home, attempting to ignore the fear that filled up my belly and tightened my chest.

On December 8, 2016, my doctor surgically removed the quarter centimeter inconvenience from my life. After the surgery, he told my husband and me that there had been a lot of bleeding because the polyp was very large and fibrous. He looked concerned but sounded hopeful. I wanted to get out of that hospital as quickly as possible, so I did not pay much attention to his concerned expression. I was sent home with the expected seven days of complete vocal rest. No talking at all.

After My Surgery

Seven days later, I returned to UCLA for my first vocal therapy appointment, as planned. I had anticipated that the first seven days of this inconvenience would be over now. I would be able to talk again, even if it was just a little bit. To be honest, I actually hoped that I was strong enough to be the exception and that my incredible recovery would dazzle the vocal therapist and the doctors at UCLA, not to mention my team and Mo-Mentum Fitness members. I actually hoped and believed that I would be back to my life within a couple of weeks after my surgery because that was what I perceived a "strong woman" would be able to do. That was my plan, but my first appointment did not go as I had anticipated.

Vocal therapists must have a good sense of humor because they have to ask people to make funny sounds all day long. After she introduced herself to me and I introduced myself by writing on my white board, she asked me to make a humming sound. She hummed in a soft, clear, pretty tone, so I could mimic her. When I began to imitate her sound, a choppy, sandpaper-like noise came out of my throat instead. Immediately, tears streamed down my face. I was embarrassed. This was not strong. The nagging little fear I had been trying to ignore was coming true.

As soon as my vocal therapist heard the sound my vocal cords produced, she told me the session had to stop. Any talking at this point would cause more harm to my vocal cords. She called the doctor and marched me next door to his office. He was ready for us when we walked in. This was a red flag since I was accustomed to waiting for him. He ushered us into the room with the camera wand. He looked down my throat at my vocal cords and then promptly walked out of the room. This was another a red flag. I knew something was wrong. I was confused. My recovery was supposed to be impressively strong, but this was not what was happening. So far, everyone looked more concerned than impressed.

My doctor returned with another doctor and a woman who began taking notes. Both doctors looked down my throat at my vocal cords again. They murmured as they looked in my throat, but I was fighting down my fear, and I could not understand them. Finally, my doctor started talking.

The polyp that had grown on my vocal cord had been there for a long time, which had allowed it to become very large and fibrous. This probably contributed to the hemorrhage inside my vocal cord as the polyp was removed. Hemorrhaging during a vocal cord surgery is extremely uncommon. The word "uncommon" was not being used as I had anticipated just a few hours earlier. Instead, I had fallen into the "uncommon and not good" category.

Hemorrhaging in a vocal cord can lead to irreversible scarring. Scarred vocal cords cannot produce an audible voice. Normal, healthy vocal cords vibrate when you talk, and the result is a smooth voice. My blood-filled (post-hemorrhaged) vocal cord could not vibrate, so it produced a sound that was more like a walrus than a human.

In a tone that did not convey the confidence he intended to impart, my doctor told me that my voice would eventually be "fine." My vocal therapist knew that the word "fine" did not sit well with me. She told me this would be REALLY tragic if I were an opera singer, but that I would eventually be able to talk again. When I asked them what my voice would sound like when I could talk again, the other doctor and the notetaker looked away, and my doctor and vocal therapist stumbled for the right words to say. Eventually, they came up with, "We don't know."

My heart dropped, and for a moment I thought I was going to throw up. My doctor and vocal therapist were trying to keep me calm, but I had heard the sound that was supposed to be my voice. I recognized the look of concern on their faces, and I knew it meant they were not sure if my voice would work again. I had literally lost my voice, and no one knew for sure what would happen next.

I left the doctor's office that morning in a slight state of shock and with a prescription of a minimum of four more weeks of COMPLETE vocal rest. This meant NO TALKING AT ALL, no humming, no clearing my throat, no coughing, and no laughing out loud. It meant that when my husband walked in our front door at home, I could NOT say, "Hi honey!" It meant no talking to my kids, even when they needed to hear my voice. When a prospect walked through the doors of my business, complete vocal rest meant I could not say, "Hello! Welcome. How can I help you?" It meant that my team would have to help me cover my group fitness classes and training sessions because a trainer who could not talk could not help her clients. It meant that every face-to-face conversation required that I write my end of that conversation on an electronic whiteboard. Complete vocal rest meant that I would spend hours texting messages to communicate with my family, team, and clients.

Conversations that would normally take three minutes orally, took fifteen minutes with a white board or text. Perhaps more importantly, complete vocal silence was accompanied by an underlying, constant feeling of isolation.

During my silence, I continued participating in the activities of my normal life. I worked at my studio every day. I went to Starbucks to get my coffee. I went to the grocery store. I used body language and my white board to communicate with people all day long. I felt loved, and even people I did not know were extremely helpful. Even still, something was missing in a conversation that was texted, typed, or written on a board. The barriers of conversation that I experienced inevitably made me appreciate the magic that happens when people can communicate orally, face to face.

We use our voices to express who we are and to highlight our emotions. For example, when you are happy, your voice may be more bouncy and playful. When you are serious, your voice may be deeper and more streamlined. When your child is sad and you are comforting her, you choose a soft tone of voice that wraps her with your love. Fluctuations in the tone of your voice during a conversation or while telling a story help to bring a story to life.

In my case, my voice was a vital part of my mission. I talk to people on a daily basis, and I enjoy presenting on stage as well. I use my voice to lead my team and my business. My voice has always been a vital part of being a mother, a wife, a daughter, and a friend. I was suddenly faced with the question of who I would become without my voice. I was lost, uncomfortable, frustrated, and admittedly, scared.

Strangely, though, even as I was absorbing all of this, I had a sense of calm underlying my fear. I had been in this uncertain place before in my life—the place where I did not know what was going to happen next. As a single mother with twins and even as a female business owner, I had overcome many struggles. As difficult as these types of situations had been, I became a stronger woman because of them. My life taught me that my attitude, beliefs, and actions are not only responsible for my end of my problems but also the solutions to those problems.

Taking Responsibility

Though I had been sharing my beliefs with my clients, members, and anyone who would listen, I had slipped away from following my own advice. I had allowed a 0.25-centimeter polyp to "be the boss of me," instead of looking at my own actions. I had not allowed myself to consider the reality of losing my voice until I had lost it. I had convinced myself that I had to ignore my failing voice because I was on a mission to build my business that would help more people. How could this be bad?

The reality was, I had pushed my vocal cords to the point of serious injury and then waited too long to correct the problem. I had been afraid of the solution, and I was making decisions about my life based on fear, and not courage.

On December 15, 2016, I walked out of my doctor's office not knowing if I would ever get my voice back. I accepted 100% responsibility. This was not a punishment, and it did not mean that the polyp was my fault. Instead, accepting 100% responsibility for my part in the loss of my voice released me from being a victim of this circumstance and empowered me to take charge of the solution.

I believe we have all experienced profound moments in our lives when we realize we are in a bad situation. Although bad situations are uncomfortable and often painful, when your back is against the wall, you really have only two options. One is to allow your circumstances to determine the direction of your life. The other is to evaluate the situation, take 100% responsibility for your part, and take immediate action towards solving your problem.

It had become very clear to me that if I did not place taking care of my body and my vocal cords before anything else in my life, I had absolutely no chance of getting my voice back. I was not a victim. I was in charge of the solution.

Spotlight Focus

As humans, we have only a finite amount of energy to use for navigating through each day. It was time to admit that I was human, and not Wonder Woman. Beating myself up over past mistakes and worrying about things that had not actually happened yet would waste that already limited energy.

On my way home from my first doctor appointment, Tony Robbins' quote popped into my head, "Where focus goes, energy flows."

The human brain is organized to act on what we expect will happen next. Focusing on what we fear concentrates our energy on what we are afraid of like a spotlight on a dark stage. If your spotlight is focused on what you fear, that is all your brain can see because everything else is dark. The human brain cannot tell the difference between reality and what we perceive is real. If you do not believe me, close your eyes and picture running the edge of a piece of paper over your tongue so you get a paper cut. OUCH! You can feel it even though it only happened in your brain! Our brains are comprised of millions of neurons communicating with each other. What we focus on in our imagination actually creates the same patterns between the same neurons that would be initiated if the event had actually occurred.

There was a possibility that I would not get my voice back, but more importantly, it was possible that my vocal cords would heal beautifully. I chose to shine my spotlight focus ONLY on the possibility of my vocal cords healing beautifully. I consciously decided to NOT allow myself to entertain the possibility of not getting my voice back. Thoughts of my vocal cords healing like twisted toothpicks and in beds of scar tissue popped in my head every day. I replaced every fearful thought with the opposite thought and action. When I envisioned myself with a walrus voice, I practiced the very rudimentary vocal drills my therapist had assigned to me. When the drills sounded bad (and they sounded very bad for a very long time), I listened for the one tiny sound I could make that most closely resembled a smooth human voice. I focused on that sound.

Every day I pictured myself on a stage talking to people again. When people asked me how I was doing I wrote on my Boogie Board, "Excellent! My voice is coming back, slowly but surely." I wrote these words, even when I felt afraid that it was not true. I wrote these words with the energy that conveyed confidence. I made myself smile as I wrote the words. I showed up early to every vocal therapy appointment. I practiced my drills five times a day just like my vocal therapist prescribed. My actions followed my focus.

To ensure that I would not re-create the same vocal cord problem when my voice came back, I let my team know that I would have to make changes in the way I taught my classes and trained my clients. I began giving my classes to my trainers. I made lists of the questions I was asked most often, so I could make videos and write blogs with the answers. I scheduled times in my days where I would rest my vocal cords and work on writing instead of talking. I did this while I was still on complete vocal rest to keep my brain focused like a spotlight on what I knew could happen.

Surround Yourself with People Who Have Your Back

Despite my focus and all of my actions towards what was possible, my second doctor's visit, 29 (silent) days later was disheartening. The bruising on my vocal cord from the hemorrhage had dissipated by about 75%, which was good, but it was still too injured to vibrate like a normal vocal cord. Again, my doctor struggled to find the words to tell me that my voice might come back just fine . . . but maybe not.

Once again, I left the doctor's office in a slight state of shock with instructions to remain on complete vocal rest until my next appointment. My confidence was shaken. I felt like I had failed my team who were all covering my classes, training sessions, and many of my responsibilities that required a voice. I felt like I had let my kids and my husband down. They were all waiting for good news from me that day, but instead I was going to have to ask for more help. As I was driving home from UCLA, I struggled to keep my mind focused on the positive. My heart felt broken. I wondered if I had the strength to continue to be positive.

By the next morning fear had taken over. I was supposed to be at Mo-Mentum, but all I really wanted to do was crawl under my desk and cry, and maybe eat some dark chocolate. As a leader, my responsibility was to show up and inspire, not to mope around. I was tired, and my fear felt greater than my strength. I was overcome by the question, "What if my vocal cords are too scarred to ever work again?"

I was not willing to become a victim of my circumstances, but on this morning, I needed reinforcements. I texted a close friend and mentor, Kelli. She said just what I needed to hear—that I could do this—that I had whatever I needed within me—and that I would be okay. Her words centered me. Within minutes, my heart had risen from my bellybutton back to my chest. I let go of my fears, regained my spotlight focus, and was fueled to inspire. Having a community of people who have your back is a vital part of living a strong life. Even more importantly, we must practice the courage it takes to be vulnerable and ask for help.

It took 63 days for my vocal cord to begin vibrating so that I could produce a smooth voice. Even after I regained my voice, I had to re-learn to talk in a new softer voice, so I would not re-create the same problem. My vocal therapist called this new voice "level 2," a relaxed, quiet voice. In terms of vocal volume "level 5" would be yelling and "level 4" would be the volume you use to talk in a loud bar. I had lived at levels 4 and 5 for over 20 years.

Talking in a quiet, softer voice was very difficult for me. It was not difficult physically. In fact, talking in a quieter, softer volume was much easier on my already traumatized vocal cords. It made complete sense. My struggle was internal. Somehow, I felt less strong, less like a leader, less like a strong businesswoman, and less like Wonder Woman.

What I learned through this experience is that a strong life does not transpire in a straight line. It is possible that even though you have done

63

everything "right" in your life, you will be blindsided by uncontrollable circumstances. I was blindsided when I lost my voice. Even though I knew for over two years that I was pushing my vocal cords too hard, I ignored my own health. I ignored the signals my body was sending me to stop what I was doing, and I mistook that for strength. I viewed my failing vocal cords as a weakness, and I was afraid that weakness meant I was letting people down.

I now recognize that in life, there is fear and there is love. Facing fear takes courage, and courage is fueled by love. You are strong when you face the things that scare you. Taking care of your body, your mind, and your spirit, so you can inspire, motivate, and make a positive impact in this world requires strength, and that strength comes from love.

I still drive to the busy coffee shop two blocks from UCLA Medical Center. I no longer dream of the opportunity to write; instead I make time to write. The obstacles in my life have become opportunities. Finding my voice allowed me to rediscover what is really important in life and to remember that taking care of myself is important and that ultimately it is the ability to love others and to love yourself that creates a strong life.

ACTION STEP

Change your evaluation of life's obstacles.

Instead of asking yourself, "Why do these things happen to me?" ask yourself these five questions:

1. What am I supposed to learn from this obstacle?

2. What is my part and what can I do differently?

3. What can I focus on to resolve this problem and end up on top?

4. Who can help me get through this?

5. How can I solve this problem through the lens of love?

No matter where you are in your life today, you can make the choice to live a strong life.

About Amanda Mittleman

With more than 20 years of experience in the fitness industry, Amanda Mittleman is a passionate, highly trained exercise physiologist, personal trainer, writer, and speaker. She is the creator of Mo-Mentum Fitness, the first studio in Huntington Beach, California, to successfully blend group fitness with personalized training to create fun, metabolic, and movement enhancement programs. Built around an empowering and upbeat culture, Mo-Mentum Fitness is one of the top performing fitness studios in Orange County.

Many of us find ourselves in a world where human movement has become increasingly dysfunctional and a source of pain due to the long hours of sitting required by our careers and due to the nature of American culture. In response Amanda developed personal and group training programs to restore functional movement while simultaneously creating a significant metabolic effect. Amanda's programming, referred to as "the party" by her clients, is light-hearted but powerful. She believes wholeheartedly that if exercise isn't fun and effective, it won't become a lifelong habit.

Amanda began her path in the fitness industry as a 25-year-old single mother of twins, who were not expected to survive past the age of 2.

She found strength in the positive community inherent within personal training sessions and group fitness classes. She earned her Master of Science in Kinesiology and Exercise Science from California State University, Long Beach, and has presented her own research and fitness workshops in many cities across the US.

In 2016, Amanda was named the Todd Durkin Fitness Professional of the Year. She was also one of three finalists for the 2015 and 2016 International IDEA Personal Trainer of the Year Award.

Passionate about helping fitness professionals create successful careers in one of today's most indispensible callings, Amanda taught a course at CSULB for aspiring undergraduate students in the kinesiology program. She also serves as an active member of the IDEA Health and Fitness Association Program Committee where she works with fellow fitness business owners from all over the world to help determine the highest quality continuing education programs for fitness professionals.

Amanda and her husband Steve combined their families 15 years ago to become a total of six. Steve often describes the family—Sumner, Samantha, Stephanie, Tyler, himself, and Amanda—as a combination of *The Brady Bunch* and *The Munsters*.

Amanda Mittleman, MS

Mo-Mentum Fitness, CEO

http://www.mo-mentumfitness.com

Instagram: AmandaMittleman

Facebook: @AmandaMittleman

CHAPTER 5

Fueling the Fire Within

by Christine Parker

Be fearless in the pursuit of what sets your soul on fire.
— Jennifer Lee

I want you to direct your attention to your breath, your center of life. Are you breathing slowly or quickly? Are you breathing through your nose or through your mouth? Breathing is something that we do every minute of every day, yet we seldom bring awareness to it. For now, I just want you to take a moment to clear your mind and focus on your own breath. Feel your abdominal wall expand with each inhale and hollow with each exhale. Focus on slowing your breath and breathing a little deeper.

As things around us continue to move faster and faster in our world, we must intentionally take moments to slow down, quiet our minds, and breathe deeply. There have been tremendous changes in technology, the environment, and lifestyles over the past 25 years. While some of it adds convenience and efficiency to our lives, it can also add stress and disconnection. Often it is hard to find the time to quiet our mind, to be still, and to breathe deeply. That is why we must make the time. It is when we turn off the electronics, silence the chatterbox in our heads, and focus our energy on ourselves that we can really connect with the strength, power, and truth that is deep inside of us. In our quiet moments, we can hear what our heart and soul are speaking and allow them to guide us. Within our mind, heart, and spirit the ultimate strength lies.

There is an inner fire in each and every one of us that has enough energy to ignite the universe. It takes fuel to build a strong fire. At times, when our fires burn low, we are left feeling empty and isolated. I know. I've been there. As a wife, mom of 4 daughters, business owner, entrepreneur, and person who is invested in a profession that is responsible for helping to change the lives of others, it is no surprise that a lot of my time is spent trying to add fuel to other people's fires. This opportunity is always a gift, yet in life, it is essential to make sure that our own fire remains lit in the process. We all know if we give too much of our own fuel without replenishing it, we will end up on empty. Nothing runs well on empty.

To live strong we must keep our fuel tank full and our fire burning! It is important that we discover what fuels our fire and that we work to develop the practices necessary to keep it burning strong. Sometimes that fire roars, and sometimes it simmers. I will share some of the things that have helped me to keep my fire burning through different seasons of life in attempt to help you to discover maybe just one new way to add fuel to your fire.

If you feel your flame burning low, the quickest and easiest way to fuel it is to add oxygen—slow down and breathe deeply.

PASSION

Passion is energy. Feel the power that comes
from focusing on what excites you.
— Oprah Winfrey

When we do something that we are passionate about, it gives us energy. Passion is that feeling, that inner high, that you get inside when you are doing something that you love. Knowing what we are truly passionate about is not always obvious, even to ourselves.

Thinking about my own journey through life, I can say that working to discover what I am passionate about has been a great source of energy and direction in life. You might expect, as an expert in the health and wellness industry, that I have a deep passion for fitness. While the statement holds some truth, it is not so black and white. Let me explain. I have a passion for helping others. I believe in the power of fitness and healthy living to assist in that, and I know its ability to change lives. I have experienced this first-hand in my own life, my clients' lives, and the lives of many that I love.

Contrary to popular belief, there are many of us in the fitness industry who do not have an overwhelming desire to wake up early, exercise, and eat right every single day! There are days that eating clean, exercising, and getting out of bed is a struggle. I do not always love working out, but I do love the fuel that I get from it in the feeling that comes afterwards. I feel accomplished, focused, and energized, and I know that my body and mind are healthier and happier because of it.

Some of the things that I am passionate about are teaching and creating movement, and learning about the effects of diet and exercise on the mind, music, cooking, and creating. These are all a part of fitness and healthy living. When I put the focus where my passions lie, my energy increases, as well as my happiness. Learning to focus on what I enjoy taught me that when we let our passions guide us, and we commit to putting our best foot forward, we gather the energy we need to live a meaningful and happy life.

DREAM

Winners, I'm convinced, imagine their dreams first.
They want it with all of their heart and expect it to come true.

— Joe Montana

What is your wildest dream? If you could be anything, do anything, live anywhere, what would it be? Dreams have the ability to light our souls on fire! I remember as a little girl, standing on top of the living room coffee table and dancing and singing to Madonna's "Like a Virgin" with absolutely no idea of what that meant. All I knew was that I was the star of the show and that this girl was on fire! I loved making people smile and feel good, and I dreamed of performing as a way to do that.

Dreaming is essential. When we are young, we dream about what we will be when we grow up. We dream about where we will live and what our lives will look like. I believe that those dreams can be a subconscious calling to a path where we can discover our gifts and become masters of them. If we take the time and discipline to develop our gifts, they will lead us on a greater path to who and what we are meant to be. Following a dream does not always move us down the path that we expect, but it, no doubt, will move us towards the person that we are meant to be!

Dreams can change throughout our journey in life. Often dreams need to change direction as we grow. As we get older, we grow more aware of challenges that may be present on the road to pursuing a dream or the changes that must be made in order to achieve our dreams. These challenges can stop us in our tracks. Sometimes something or someone in life discourages our dreams. Dreaming and recognizing all that it takes to make a dream happen can be a very scary thought. If we let fear overtake us and we stop dreaming, we run the risk of letting our fire burn out.

Dreaming BIG often requires us to look at things in a new way. It requires change! When we dream big, we must let go of things that are not serving us and develop new habits that will help us grow to become the person that can achieve our dreams. It takes time to dream! Every one of us deserves a chance to dream BIG and pursue the path to our dreams, for that is what adds fuel to our fire.

FEAR

Let your dreams BE BIGGER than your fears.
Fear regret more than failure.

When I was young, I had a dream to dance. During recitals, dance competitions, and performances, my mother was always my biggest fan, but like most parents, she hated to see my disappointment when things did not come out the way that I desired. She saw the ups and downs of competitions and auditions and how so many other girls were out there going after a similar dream. When I expressed my desire to pursue dance as a career, she was not on board. My mom reminded me how hard it would be to make a living with a career in dance. What if I got injured? Where would I find a job? How would I pay my bills? She was afraid that as a dancer I would constantly have to deal with this cycle of hope, anticipation, and rejection. My mom tried to send me on a detour to other paths that she believed would be better for me to follow.

It was not that my mom did not think I was good. She loved to watch me dance, and in her "mom eyes" I was always amazing. She wanted me to be happy and do what I loved, but she was passing along her fear of a world that she did not know. She feared my ability to handle the challenges that would lie ahead on this unknown path, and she was not sure that she could help me. When I faced failure and disappointment, so did she. She did not want to see me hurt and hated to see me take the hard road when she thought there was one that might be a little safer and more secure.

As a parent, it is so hard to see our children fail and suffer, but fear is the number one barrier between us and our ability to truly live our dreams. Fear will extinguish our inner fire in minutes. Some of the most common fears are fear of failure, fear of not being good enough, fear of taking that first step, fear of stepping out of our comfort zone, fear of having to sacrifice, and fear of our own ability to succeed. Sometimes we come up with excuses that perpetuate our fears: "There is not enough time," "It is not the right time," "I do not have enough money," "I am not ready yet," "I do not have the same opportunity as everyone else." These are all excuses that hold us back. When we make excuses, we take away the opportunity to experience failure and in that, we also take away the opportunity for growth. Fear can keep us in a comfortable place, yet it can also short-circuit our lives and our ability to reach our true potential.

What I have learned is that fear can drain us or it can become a constant source of fuel. I remember reading a book years ago titled *Feel the Fear and Do It Anyway* by Susan Jeffers. This book was a life-changer for me.

It made me realize how much my fear was controlled by my thinking and how much control I actually had over fear. It helped me to understand where my fear was coming from. As a result, I learned a new way to approach fear in my life. Asking myself a few simple questions in the face of fear has helped me to push past my fears, test my limits, and step out of my comfort zone.

1.   Do I want this more than I am afraid of it?

2.   Will I regret this if I do not do it?

3.   Will this matter in 1 year, 3 years, 5 years?

4.   What is the worst thing that can happen and can I live with that?

These four questions have helped me to overcome many fears and make decisions in some of my most challenging moments.

As I continue to grow, I continue to face new fears. I have learned that one of the biggest ways to conquer fear is to take action!

TAKING ACTION

A tiny spark can set a great forest on fire.
— James 3:5

We can dream about what we want, but until we decide to take action and take the steps necessary to achieve our dreams, they remain just dreams! One of the most important principles that dance provided at a young age was an appreciation for discipline and the opportunity to develop it. I had the chance to learn that reward had to be earned through hard work. It was humbling to see an outstanding artist because there was an understanding of the amount of time and dedication that was necessary to transform a body into a vessel, which could make the most difficult feats look effortless.

I vividly remember in my dance career, my first contract with Holland America Line cruises. There was a one-month rehearsal period in Pasadena, California, during which we spent 8–10 hours a day dancing, memorizing choreography, rehearsing songs, and practicing costume changes and staging cues. After four weeks of grind, we excitedly boarded the ship for what was known as "hell week." I still have nightmares about that week! We spent seven days rehearsing and staging the shows in the middle of the night while the passengers were sleeping. During the day we had costume fittings, ship orientations, and crew drills. I was young, so my experience with sacrificing things like sleep, personal time, and meals was all quite new. Along with the crazy schedule we were learning to turn, leap, balance, and tumble in 3-inch heels aboard a moving vessel, and we practiced completing costume and wig changes in 90 seconds or less with the help of the Indonesian and Filipino stage crew. Put that together with a disrupted sleep pattern, slight exhaustion, and seasickness, and welcome to "hell week." This was not the initial vision that I had of life aboard a cruise ship and being a star of the show!

No matter how hard you work, you do not always get the reward that you are looking for when you are looking for it. Your actions and hard work will continue to provide opportunities that will move you forward on the journey. We must learn and be willing to embrace the process and recognize that there are lessons and skills to be learned in each and every situation in life. Sometimes the reward that we anticipate does not ever happen. In those moments, the lessons learned become the reward. It is through this process that we learn, grow, and gain our greatest ability to live strong. "Hell" week was unexpected. It may not have been exactly what I anticipated when I decided to work on that cruise, but the action

I took gave me a chance to learn. My life is stronger because of that experience.

Have Gratitude and Embrace the Journey

It is good to have an end to journey towards;
but it is the journey that matters, in the end.
— Ernest Hemingway

Do you ever look back at pictures and say, "Those were the days"? Why is it that we often do not realize that these are the days when we are living them? What about when you feel like you are at your wits' end, and someone comes up to you and advises, "Appreciate these days. They will be gone before you know it"? Sometimes it takes everything inside not to throw them a right hook when deep down you know that they are right! Some day you will look back and yearn for this day again.

Fortunately, having four children has granted me a few extra gray hairs and some opportunities to appreciate moments with my younger children that I never quite fully embraced with my older ones. I am learning to be grateful for the little things, to let go of the things that are not important, and to better embrace the journey. It is not always easy, for embracing the journey doesn't just mean the great parts; it also means having gratitude for the challenges and the parts that are not so pretty!

As with all things, we get better with practice. We know that life on earth comes with struggles and rough patches. These moments remind us to slow down and reevaluate what is important in our lives, the purpose of our lives, and the quality of our lives. Embracing the journey requires faith. It requires faith in what we cannot see and cannot control.

76

We need to trust that what we cannot see or control will work out the way that it is meant to be and learn to surrender ourselves to the present moment.

How many times do we set our eyes on something and decide that we want it NOW? If success does not happen in a week or a month or a year, then it is time to throw in the towel. This happens with careers, with relationships, and with life goals. There is not one giant leap to the top. Overnight success is pretty much a myth. It is said to take 10,000 hours to become a "master" at something, and for most people that equates to about 10 years of life. That is a long time! When you recognize the many monumental moments that can happen in that time, then you can begin to appreciate the journey and everything in it.

To keep our tank full, we must take time to be grateful for the daily blessings and celebrate the small victories along the way. It is no coincidence that those who do not give up often find success in life. We must keep taking small steps and have faith that they are leading us in the right direction. When we make time to have daily gratitude and embrace all parts of the journey, we will attract more of what we need and want into our days, and we create a meaningful life along the way.

Invest in Yourself

> *Invest in yourself now and reap dividends day*
> *after day after month after year.*
> — Jack LaLanne

It would not be right if I did not include a section about health and wellness in my chapter. This is, after all, a book filled with health and wellness experts! There are many components to living strong and keeping our fire fueled. Having great day-to-day energy is one of the cornerstones of being able to live life to the fullest, and our health and fitness have a tremendous effect on our daily energy. Health and fitness do not just impact how our bodies work, but they have a huge influence on how our minds work as well.

We all have that little voice in our head that sneaks out to remind us of our insecurities, overwhelm us, cause anxiety at times, and attempt to defuel our fire. In life, there are a lot of things that cannot be controlled. Exercise and our nutrition are two things that we do have control over. What is so exciting about that is that exercise and nutrition have a direct effect on how our bodies move, how they feel, and also on that sneaky little voice inside of our heads.

Inflammation in our bodies, which is the root of disease and the cause of injury and pain, can be greatly affected by our exercise and nutrition habits. If we want our bodies to move and feel better, then we need to look at our exercise and nutrition as an opportunity to work as medicine on our bodies and minds. In the case of the mind, one of the ways exercise promotes mental health is by normalizing insulin resistance and boosting natural "feel good" hormones and neurotransmitters associated with mood control, including endorphins, serotonin, dopamine, glutamate, and GABA. What we eat also greatly impacts the structure and function of our brain.

Our energy, the state of our mind, and the ability for our body to function properly and feel strong are all priceless. I have gone through periods in my life when I have battled through depression and health issues related with anemia. I know what it is like to have a body that does not feel good and a mind that races out of control. In my younger years, I was prescribed antidepressants. As I learned the science behind exercise and nutrition, and experienced its effects on my own body and mind, I understood the need for it in my life and the importance of creating healthy habits. My life truly depended on it! Exercise and creating healthy lifestyle habits have been two of the key components that have carried me through these times. It is part of the journey that I have embraced and now have the desire to pass along. That is not to say that there is not a need for medication and that certain situations do not require it, but I believe that we need to take responsibility with the role that we can play on the state of our body and our mind as well!

I am in the health and fitness industry, and I know that making ourselves, our fitness, and our nutrition a priority can be exceptionally challenging, especially when mixed with the day-to-day responsibilities of life and taking care of the needs of others. Taking care of ourselves is not optional. When we do not pay attention to what our body needs physically, nutritionally, and spiritually, it will eventually take a toll on us.

We have been granted one body and one life, so find gratitude! We must take the time to discover and appreciate the gifts that we have to share and to understand what truly brings us happiness in our life. It is a journey! Be fearless in your pursuit to live out your dreams and share your gifts with others while embracing the good and bad along the way. Be persistent in creating good habits and making the time for the things that will help you to be the best version of yourself. There is truly no better investment for you and those around you than the investment that you make in yourself!

ACTION STEP

*Which area of your life, discussed in this chapter,
do you most need to improve?*

Do you need to find some time to dream?

Do you need to rediscover your passion?

Is fear overwhelming you?

Do you need to make time for gratitude?

Or is it time to focus on improving your exercise and nutritional habits?

Then start moving forward. When you do, you will fuel your inner fire!

ABOUT CHRISTINE PARKER

Every day is an opportunity to learn something new about ourselves and the world that surrounds us, and it is through our most challenging endeavors that we build our deepest layers of strength.

— Christine Parker

Christine Parker is the owner of FitHouse, a wife, and a mother of four beautiful daughters. She is deeply dedicated to helping others find empowerment by building strong and healthy bodies and minds.

Christine grew up in Pittsburgh, PA, where dance and gymnastics were a big part of her childhood. She had a dream to dance on stage and earned a scholarship to Point Park College where she majored in dance and minored in psychology. From a young age, Christine was passionate about the connection of the body, mind, and spirit.

Following that passion led her to Los Angeles and a career in dance. She is grateful for all of the experiences, opportunities, and people that she met there who helped her learn early on that hard work, discipline, and the ability to overcome failure could lead to great things.

Christine has been influenced by some of the top fitness professionals in the industry: Todd Durkin, Peter Twist, Martin Rooney, and Mindy Mylrea, to name a few. She is a member of the IDEA Health and Fitness Association, a Platinum member of the Todd Durkin Mastermind Institute, a nationally certified personal trainer through ISSA and NASM, and a nationally certified group fitness instructor through AFFA.

Additional certifications and coursework include TRX, BOSU, Precision Nutrition, and Prenatal and Post-Natal Fitness.

She is blessed to have a husband, children, and family who support and believe in her vision and bring her love and happiness each and every day.

Christine Parker BFA Dance, CPT, CES

Owner, FitHouse

www.fithousepa.com

Instagram: @Fithouse_pa

Facebook: @Fithousepa

CHAPTER 6

MIND, BODY . . . GAME

by Christa Pryor

Two years ago, a blue-eyed, freckled, 12-year-old soccer athlete walked into the gym. Though her mom and I had spoken, it was important for me to speak with her individually. In my time training young athletes I had encountered both hovering parents and kids trying to please their parents, so I wanted to know who I was working with.

She extended her hand, and introduced herself as Sierra. When asked why she wanted to work with me, Sierra took a contemplative breath, looked me in the eye, and replied, "The girls I play with are a year older than me, so I am undersized. I need to be faster. I want to build a stronger core and upper body, so I can push girls off the ball." There was no hesitation in her voice. She was resolute, and I was taken aback. If her physical ability matched the astute self-awareness that she just shared, she was going to be a whole lot of fun, and this was going to be one hell of a ride.

As weeks and months rolled past, I began to understand what a student of the game Sierra truly was. She did not just watch games, she studied them. She visualized herself blazing past her opponents, and every weekend she fired off a barrage of PKs and corner kicks. She spent "days off" in her backyard trying to break her juggling record—1,617 touches to date.

One Monday afternoon this past February, Sierra came bounding into the gym, her smile eclipsing the setting sun behind her. She greeted me with her usual, "Hi Christa," hugging my waist. But this time, her enveloping arms were electric with her exuberance.

Feeling her infectious joy, I looked down at her and asked how her tournament went over the weekend.

She beamed, "Amazing."

The next few minutes were filled with a flurry of words: her play-by-play illustrating the moves she tried for the first time, the girls peeling off her as she attacked the field, and the PK that sailed into the box. Her colorful commentary was stacking blocks of mini-milestones, each one reinforcing a heightened self-assuredness. "Coach kept saying that he wanted me to take more risks, to be more aggressive, and I finally did it!"

The week before she had mentioned she felt her coaches were more critical of her than her teammates. I had suggested that perhaps the reason she received the feedback was that they trusted that she was mature enough to handle it.

They knew that she would hear it, absorb it, and then work to make the changes to improve, respectfully. They knew she wanted to be the best athlete she could. Now, she was before me, vibrating on the power that she had tapped into from this breakthrough.

As we progressed through her session that day, I observed a new tenacity as Sierra executed her drills. Her success on the field had carried over into her work with me. She found the courage to play with vulnerability, and her reward was a sensation of accomplishment, invigoration, and pride. In this moment, I had an epiphany ...

When I first learned of the opportunity to be a contributing writer for this book, I was eager to apply. I have always fancied myself a writer. I have one novel yet to be finished and have toyed with children's books in the past. However, once I learned of the topic, I hesitated. Who was I to talk about the best practices of how to live your best life?

When I sat down to write, I struggled to find the words to begin. I would sit down at the computer and within minutes I was researching body butter recipes. I would find my focus until I wanted a cup of tea, and then I was re-organizing kitchen cabinets. I rearranged the furniture, twice.

Why was I struggling? I was bewildered. I wrote all the time as a child. I came to the conclusion that I was afraid to see what would happen when I started to go deep.

What would be revealed? That I wanted more in life? That I knew that I was capable of doing so much more?

I took a breath, pushed away from the table once again, but this time I took a moment to reflect ...

I had been here before. It is like having to stick your naked foot in an ice bucket to treat a sprained ankle. You know it is going to reduce the swelling and help you get back on the court, but the first 30 seconds are painful and so nauseating, it might be better if you could just pass out from the shock. That is a metaphor for life. Time and again we are given a choice to play it safe or to step into courage. Here I was, presented with an opportunity to sit on the bench, cheer from the sideline, or step onto the field and ask for the ball. It was all a part of the game, and I was going to play.

As a college athlete, I struggled. I was not happy with the way I was playing, I was not happy with my team. It seemed that even if I put up extra shots or more hours in the weight room, it was not making a difference on the court.

One day, a thought entered my mind: how is it that some people always seem to "win"? What is that little something extra? I could not define it. Truthfully, I did not have the awareness to understand what "it" was or how to get "it." However, I knew enough to know that I was missing "it." In my mind, it seemed like an equation:

Elevate the Mind + Elevate the Body = Elevate the Game

Over time, I have realized that it is not so much an equation as a formula. This formula is one that transcends the athletic arena and can be embraced as a philosophy for life.

Elevate the Mind

When I first came up with the notion of elevating the mind, I knew that it was important but its true significance eluded me. I think that I was disillusioned. My deepest dreams were muted by the notions of setting goals, making plans, trying to build visions of what I was supposed to do. But these goals were shallow. There was nothing to anchor them because they were not aligned with who I was.

By happenstance, I was moving in a direction of self-discovery. My subconscious was attracting opportunities that spoke to who I was at my core, opportunities that exposed me to creative people in the arts and athletics, and afforded me the chance to travel. My intuition had found a way to guide me even though I was so disconnected.

It was during my travels that I began to explore the art of meditation. I was experiencing anxiety attacks and had read somewhere that meditation could help relieve its symptoms. My friend Steve, who had been practicing for some time, encouraged me to "start with five minutes." It felt like five hours. I could not keep my body still, let alone my mind. As a child, I had a strong affinity for Tigger from *Winnie the Pooh*, and I was beginning to understand why.

I kept trying new things—letting the thoughts just float in and out of my mind, looking at a candle flame, closing my eyes . . . Each day I found some success, but nothing that made me feel confident I could sustain stillness for 20 minutes. I experimented with breathing, focusing on my breath, inhaling for three counts, exhaling for six. After a few days, I was able to sustain my stillness for 10 to 12 minutes. But I realized that sometimes I could not "get there." It felt too much like "work." I paused and reasoned that the goals for meditation, at least for me, were to decompress and restore a sense of calm when anxiety was taking hold. It occurred to me that there was nothing that centered me more than watching the sunset. From this discovery, I started trying to see the sunset or the sunrise as much as possible. Doing so created my own space and time, allowing me to collect myself. I enjoyed it so much that I started filming them so that when I started to get ahead of myself, I could still "get away."

In my exploration of meditation, I discovered that even though I was struggling to master it, I was still receiving positive effects. Meditation was like a feather duster, collecting the fragmented thoughts that veiled the windows of my soul, sweeping them aside so that things that really mattered could shine through. It was a pathway to mindfulness enabling me to sequester negative thoughts and detach myself from limiting beliefs that once held me hostage. It was calming my mind, helping me to find focus and to be present. Meditation cleared space for my mind to imagine, and as a result, my dreams began to expand and life became more colorful.

I found that my meditation practice allowed me to see different perspectives. It was as if my mind became a kaleidoscope where I had a finite set of pieces to a puzzle, but in turning the lens, I could create a completely different image and illuminate a new solution to the puzzle.

My first attempts to master this skill were in the beginning stages of my career. Originally, I had the "normal" flight path of a personal trainer working the rush hours at a gym—early in the morning to early evening—as I built my client roster. This was followed by a quick transition into the head strength and conditioning coach at a university in the Big East Conference. Though some may think coaching at a university would afford an easy "routine," it was incredibly demanding work trying to balance 10 different sports and over 300 athletes. Each team had assigned training hours while each athlete had their own individual needs and their own way of learning. Being able to see my athletes' varying perspectives aided me in becoming a more effective coach. As I became more receptive, my mind became more supple, and I learned to deliver feedback in a manner that they could receive it.

Having a supple mind proved to be invaluable when I was traveling with my first NBA athlete. Ronny Turiaf was from the island of Madinina in the French Caribbean and had asked me to train him during his summer travels in preparation for the World Basketball Championships. It was as exciting as it sounds. I traveled to different countries, worked with a myriad of professional athletes, and truly had one of the best summers of my life.

It was also tremendously challenging work. Ronny had committed to hosting and participating in several youth sports camps in the

Caribbean and South America. We did not really have a "home base." We rarely stayed in one location longer than four days. I was responsible for making sure that I kept his nutrition in check and prescribed his athletic recovery while maintaining our rigorous training schedule.

As we were so transient, I could only carry a small bag of equipment that would fit inside my backpack. My kit housed a rainbow of bands and cones, a TRX, dozens of carabiners, and it doubled as a sandbag. We trained from the beaches of the Caribbean to the jungles of the Amazon, literally. I became skilled at climbing palm trees to "MacGyver" our own special playground. Plans often changed midday requiring me to alter a training program and come up with something quickly for a completely different space.

To this day, it remains my favorite coaching experience. I was blessed to be surrounded by incredible people with vision and passion and to have the opportunity to embark upon parts of the world I had yet to discover. That summer was pre-eminent in my career. The lessons I learned from having to adapt to changing environments and cultures, as well as learning to repurpose ordinary things to fashion training equipment, have evolved into being some of my greatest strengths as a coach.

Elevate the Body

The body is a beautifully intricate machine with a menagerie of moving parts and systems that coalesce in order for it to run smoothly. But the body cannot operate without the mind. The brain is the true governor of the body. It is all interconnected. We cannot isolate one thing if we hope to achieve optimal performance.

As science continues to examine the mind-body connection, one of the emerging areas of study is neuroplasticity, which means that the brain is plastic and pliable, and just like a muscle, it will continue to develop as we use it. In fact, science has demonstrated that exercise stimulates neurogenesis, the growth of new neurons in the brain. This brilliant symbiotic relationship reinforces the idea that just as you must provide fuel for the mind, you must stimulate the body.

There was a period in my career where I spent months at a time living out of a suitcase. While I was coaching Victoria Azarenka on the WTA Tour, we might compete in three tournaments in three different cities within four weeks. Pin-balling the globe was incredibly exciting though at times a bit disruptive. Upon arriving at my hotel, one of the first things I would do was find a way to move. It eased the jet lag and offered me a chance to release some energy. More often than not, I would run. It was an easy way to get my blood pumping and recharge my batteries. More importantly, it was a constant that I could carry with me around the globe.

I can recall the first time I took the train into Lausanne, Switzerland. It was absolutely breathtaking. Admiring the lush rolling hills reflected in Lake Geneva, I could not wait to get outside.

My run was magical with the Alps in the backdrop, wildflowers sprinkling the hillside, their colors exploding below me as I stepped one foot in front of the other. It was a moving meditation. I was escaping time inside a real-life Monet painting.

As a coach, I have always been an advocate of cultivating character through sports. After all, movement was my first language. It is my vehicle for self-expression. It is how I share my excitement and how I release aggression. It was in my physical connection with my body that I first found comfort and laid the foundation for confidence. Until recently, I had aligned that sensation as an innate part of being an athlete. I had not realized the tremendous impact movement could have on someone outside of athletics. The side effects of moving your body can be visceral, emotional, and empowering.

A few years ago, I moved to San Diego to work with a family. It was a bit of a departure from what I normally do. Though I had traveled the world to work with my athletes, I had not relocated to work singularly with one family before.

It was a patriarchal household with four kids aged 12 to 21. The mother, Valerie, had not been physically active, confessing the last time she had exercised was climbing the stairs of her high school. Though I had been hired to focus on the kids, I felt she was going to be my project.

Valerie spent so much of her life taking care of her kids, driving them to games and dance recitals. I wanted her to carve out a window that was decidedly hers. We decided that every Friday morning, after dropping her daughter at school, we would drive down to the beach and go for a run.

Now understand, she welcomed the idea of going to the beach, but running . . . The first time all we did was "walk-n-talk." We progressed to running down the beach with a timer. We would jog as far as she could before she felt like she could not go any further and then walk for an equal amount of time, essentially alternating between a jog and a walk every two minutes. One day, on the back leg of our "gossip run," I turned to see that Valerie was tearing. She was in the midst of explaining why she felt like she did not contribute anything to her family. She believed people only spoke to her because she was Mark's mom or Julien's wife. Speechless, I listened.

She continued, words spilling from her mouth faster than our feet were moving. I learned that she was fearful of everything. She had been afraid to exercise. She was afraid to go places by herself. She had a pool that she had never been in because she was afraid of the water. I asked a few probing questions to see if I could get a better understanding of where she was coming from. Her fears were broad and numerous and largely out of my scope of expertise.

We walked for a while in shared silence, feeling the water tickle our toes as the tide crept in. Though her fears had been heavy, it seemed her tears had left her feeling lighter. Somewhere along the way, I giggled to myself. I had an idea. I looked at Valerie, "What if we start attacking these fears, one by one?" I pointed out that she had already broken through one barrier just in our Friday morning runs. She smiled. "Swimming's next."

Even though we had made this grand proclamation about her learning to swim, we were not ready to go at it the following day. We needed to build her up a bit more. I decided to increase the intensity of our runs. Before long she ran the entire length of the beach without stopping. It was just over a mile! I think she surprised herself. The pride on her face as we walked back to the car was a new experience for me, different from what I felt working with my athletes. I am not sure just how to explain it. It was not just pride. There was self-satisfaction.

A metamorphosis was taking place. Valerie soon became my "best athlete." She was dressing a bit differently. Her kids seemed to have a little more respect for her. She was not so easily persuaded. There was a new energy around her. Valerie could no longer slip into the room without being noticed because she had begun to take notice of herself, and everyone else followed her lead.

I posed the idea of a pool workout a few times, and I could read her trepidation and pushed it off. Then one day, after she had had logged her biggest milestone thus far, running nearly 2.5 miles without stopping, I decided it was time for the pool.

It was a beautiful day, approaching 70, and the water was in the 80s. I had a collection of pool noodles in the water. I hopped into the deepest part of the pool, so she could see that if she got spooked, all she had to do was stand up tall and she would be alright. My plan was just to get her into the pool. We were not going to start swimming that day, just walking back and forth. I wanted her to get acquainted with the water. Before I could begin my premeditated coaxing, she dropped her towel, grabbed her nose, and leapt into the water. Within seconds a roar of excitement erupted from the surface of the pool. We looked at one another and broke out in laughter.

I was awe-struck. Valerie had transformed. She was more present at home. She laughed more easily. Though she had not really lost any weight, people commented on how great she looked because she carried herself with more confidence. Her self-efficacy had grown so much that she boldly jumped right into the pool with no regard for her fear of the water.

Working with Valerie put a spotlight on the special kind of strength that comes from teaching your body how to do something new, from accepting a physical challenge and taking steps to conquer it. It is indicative of the mind-body connection, and the resilience created in the process—the determination needed to persevere through the discomfort and pain to meet fear head-on. The power that is earned by exposing your vulnerability transcends the movement and is carried over into your psyche (spirit) so that when you are faced with another challenge, you have a reserve to draw from.

Elevate the Game

To embrace the mind-body connection is not enough. We have to take action, use what we have learned, and make use of our skills and talent.

We can stand on the sidelines and cheer people on, or we can learn from Sierra and Valerie—let go of our apprehension, have the courage to be imperfect, and risk making a mistake. We can play the game.

By far, the most exciting and triumphant moments in my life have been the direct result of acting on a leap of faith. In fact, some of the most pivotal moments of my life came when I just said yes and walked into the unknown.

In 1999, my first year as a grad assistant at Boston University, one of the students from my class asked if I would like to go to see a speaker at the Hynes Convention Center. I had moved to Boston without knowing anyone, so I welcomed the opportunity to meet new people. While I was waiting for her in front of the convention center, a woman came up to me and introduced herself as a talent manager. She asked if she could take my photo. I thought it was an innocuous request, said yes, and went on about my day.

A few weeks later, Enna Kelly called to ask if I would be interested in going to New York, so she could introduce me to a few people. Flattered, I agreed. Who turns down a trip to New York City? That Friday, she picked me up and shared the itinerary. We had a few stops to make and a few different agencies she wanted to take me to. I finally started to catch a clue. I was a tomboy that did not wear a stitch of makeup and did not own a pair of heels, yet she thought I could model. I was tickled.

A few hours later we were in the city walking through the streets of SoHo, and it was brilliant. This city was vibrant. I think I was still buzzing from the stimulation of the streets of New York when I passed through the doors of Wilhelmina. I met with a man named Tom who had a charming smile and was absolutely lovely. After chatting for 30 minutes he excused himself, and I sat in the white room admiring the black and white still-life paintings on the wall. I was completely out of my head, just happy to be sitting in NYC. Returning, Tom looked at me and said that he would like to offer me a contract. WHAT? The next few moments passed in a vacuum. I walked out to Enna with a signed contract and the name and number of a photographer for my first shoot.

I began juggling grad school in Boston and shoots in New York. By the end of my second semester, the agency said that I needed to move to New York if I was going to take this seriously. I remember struggling to make a decision. My friends told me to go, but there was this side of me that was pragmatic and thought, "This isn't in the plan." Then again, who was I to walk away from an opportunity like this?

I needed to expedite my degree. I took extra classes through both summer semesters, arranged to finish my last classes as "independent study," and moved to the Big Apple.

Moving to New York was the catalyst for my life as it is now. The stories that I get to share are rooted in the woman I became after making that one decision. Living in New York opened my eyes to the world that I had not anticipated. I had always had a passion for travel, meeting new people, and exploring different cultures, and modeling afforded me the opportunity to experience it all.

But more than that, it allowed me to fully appreciate all the different sides of me—to embrace myself as a woman and to really see who I was and who I wanted to be. The people I came in contact with, the friends who became family, opened my eyes and gave me the courage to dream. I began to seek out possibilities that I honestly do not know if I would have even conceived had I not made that pivotal decision. To this day, it is the best decision that I have ever made. Ever.

Years later, after I had moved back to California, I found myself standing between two different paths yet again. I was working for a high-end gym in Los Angeles and training an athlete who asked me to go on the road to train him. It was pretty much all that I had dreamed of—a life with sports and travel; plus I would get the opportunity to help him with his kids camp—my dream trifecta!

When I asked my boss if I could take a sabbatical, her response was quick and succinct: no. In all my days I could not imagine her saying no. In my mind this would only make me a more valuable asset for the team. But she was steadfast, "If you want to train him, you have to quit." I left that day, in shock and scared for what lay ahead, but knowing that whatever it may be, wherever it might take me, it was going to be an adventure. Just as before, an act of courage, taking a risk and stepping towards the unknown, was the catalyst for a brilliant new chapter in my life.

I learned so much about myself and about the world. I was doing what I truly loved for the better part of the year and was vibrating on such a high frequency that when my contract ended and I returned home, life was difficult. I had to completely start over. I had to find a new place to live, a new job, and reestablish friendships that had been put on hold in my absence. It was one of the most overwhelming things I have ever had to do.

After my experience on the road, I came to the realization that working for a gym where I would have to have my training programs approved was not going to make me happy. I relished creative autonomy. Seemingly, the only choice was for me to branch out and begin building the ELEVATE brand—an arduous task that I was not quite prepared for, mentally or emotionally. The next few years were filled with wins and losses. There was always a new challenge to face; two new tasks to tackle for every one that I completed. When I found success, it was easy to carry that momentum onto a new project, to use that energy as fuel and inspiration.

It was an altogether different story when things did not go my way. At times, I was able to quickly brush the dirt off my shoulders and step forward without losing too much ground. But then there were other moments when the loss weighed more heavily on my psyche, dragging me across the bottom as I tried to navigate my way out of the shallows.

But, this is a part of life. It is in the moments of struggle, in the face of a challenge, that great opportunity awaits our courage. I had to call upon all of the work that I had done before, pull from my internal resources, and claw my way up from the bottom. I sought out meditation to help me find composure amidst uncertainty and clarity to create a new strategy. Running could lift my spirits and provide a spark of energy. I had everything I needed to stay in the game, I just had to play.

Elevate the Mind + Elevate the Body = Elevate the Game

Athlete or not, we are all playing a game. Life is a game of mystery and adventure. We can create a game plan for our lives down to the most finite detail, but in reality we only have so much control. Life is going to lay obstacles in our path, pepper us with distractions and pitfalls. We can do our best to prepare for what lies ahead. We must train the mind to be calm and agile to clear the hurdles, and strengthen the body to pull ourselves over obstacles. We can accept challenges and learn new skills so that we are sharp and resilient. But in order to elevate our game, we have to play.

The epiphany that I experienced as I worked with Sierra was this . . .

I had my reservations about what qualified me to contribute to this book, but I soon realized that this was just a metaphor for challenges we all face. My hesitation was rooted in mistakes of my past, impacted by myopic thinking, and thus grounded in my fears. In order to give myself a chance at winning this game, I had to be vulnerable. I had to trust my intuition, take a risk, and bet on myself.

This is perhaps the most valuable key to living your best life: when we accept life's challenges, we receive a gift of bravery. It asks us to leave footprints in the wake of trepidation and face our fears. When we choose to shrink instead of expand, we take ourselves out of the game. But when we step into our courage, we run out onto the field and call for the ball. We elevate our game.

ACTION STEP

On a piece of paper, make two columns and label them "mind" and "body."

In the first column, write out several ways that you can elevate your mind. What practices do you need to institute or continue that will help you improve your mind?

In the second column, write down several ways that you can elevate your body. What ways can you improve your physical health? Do you need to improve your exercise routine or dial in your nutrition? What can you do to make your body healthier?

At the bottom of the page, take some time to write out how the steps you listed will help elevate your game. How will the actions you take to improve your mind and body actually improve your life? Take time to write these out because these are the reasons, the why, behind the improvement. When you elevate your mind and your body, the direct result is an elevated life.

ABOUT CHRISTA PRYOR

Christa Pryor, MS, CSCS, is an elite sport performance coach, model, entrepreneur, and adventurer who educates and inspires others through her work as a leader in the sports and fitness industry. Born and raised in the San Francisco Bay Area, Christa was a 2-sport collegiate athlete, playing basketball and soccer. Her passion for sports led her to attain a bachelor's in kinesiology and a master's in human biodynamics. After receiving her graduate degree, Christa split her talents between coaching and nurturing her creative and adventurous spirit, modeling, and acting.

Christa believes that sport is an art form and the human body is her medium. Her coaching style intricately weaves traditional strength and conditioning methods with functional neurology to elevate sport performance. As an expert in the field, Christa has worked with NBA athletes, Aaron Gordon, Zach Lavine, and Andrew Wiggins; NBA champion Ronny Turiaf; WBO champion, Manny Pacquiao; tennis champion, Victoria Azarenka; and French National Footballers, Dimitri Payet and Ronny Rondelin; in addition to several other athletes in the NFL, NBA, AVP, and endurance sports. Christa continues to explore opportunities to bring ELEVATE Mind Body Game with the global (international) sports and fitness community.

Christa Pryor, MS, CSCS, NASM

ELEVATE Mind Body Game

www.ELEVATEMBG.com

www.MindBodyGame.com

IG/Twitter: @christapryor

Facebook: @christa pryor/ ELEVATE

CHAPTER 7

DECADE THINKING

by Lisa Berman

Tell me, what is it you plan to do with your one wild and precious life?
— Mary Oliver

In my first decade of life, at my little desk in Ms. Wright's first grade classroom, I sat putting sounds together to make up words and then words together to make sentences as we had learned the year before in kindergarten. This day would be my first attempt at putting sentences together to make what would become a paragraph.

My sweet, feisty, white-haired, turquoise-jewelry-adorned teacher guided us to pick a topic for our very first essay. We were to choose something we were passionate about.

I can still see the title on the manila-colored wide-lined paper in my perfectly practiced first grade penmanship:

My Grandma . . .

This was, no doubt, my biggest academic undertaking to date. We probably spent a month learning and working on this thing. As the words came together, sentences formed, and my heart poured out onto the page telling the story of a woman with a golden heart. She was, by far, one of my first favorite subjects.

I do not know why, but as I was putting my closing thoughts together that day, the realization came to me that someday ... she would not be here anymore! Overcome with emotion, I put my head down on my desk and cried into my arms. This was a pivotal realization in my first decade of life. Admittedly, I was a serious kid ... And, I just remember deciding right then to make the most of my time and deeply love the people in my life.

Somewhere in our lives we begin to think about our longevity and that of our loved ones. How long will I live? How long are we likely to have to enjoy our loved ones and to make a positive impact on the world?

When you look at the elders in your family, who are you most genetically like?

How many decades are you likely to live—60s? 70s? 80s? 90s? Beyond?

How old are you now and what are you doing to make sure you are living your personal best life? If you are 42, what are you doing to make sure you will be the best 52-year-old you can be—physically, mentally, spiritually, financially, personally, professionally, and globally?

Along my path, I started to think of life, as most of us really do, in decades. We often reference out loud and in our heads what we think of and plan to be doing in our 20s, 30s, 40s, and so on. A decade is a short enough amount of time to conceptualize but a long enough time during which to make a real difference—for better or for worse! Ten years is a long time, but the years do kind of fly by, and we only get a certain number of them. Life usually gets busier as we grow older, and time seems to fly by faster and faster.

As a wife, mom of 5 kiddos (now grown), daughter, friend, coach, and business owner with an insatiable desire to learn and grow, I found that organizing my time and thoughts had become increasingly important. I had a career I loved, and I wanted to keep kindling that fire while giving my best to the honor and challenge of being a mom.

As a child, I loved playing house and knew I wanted to be an "all-in" young mom with a big family. When I was 28, I emerged from five years being pregnant and loving every part of it! We gave birth to four babies in just about four years—No TWINS! We had three in diapers at any given time . . . all in car seats. We had the coolest limo stroller, went everywhere with the babies, and we had our hands FULL! It was not easy, but I knew I wanted to make the most of every moment, and that included being the best wife, mom, and fitness professional I could be.

Learning to be very present, while maintaining my 10,000-foot perspective became my craft and a huge part of both my family life and my profession. (I have had the opportunity to study from and train, coach, and impact top 1% leaders.)

In my mind, I break a decade down into manageable chunks that I think of as a kind of "Decade Time Pyramid." To make the most of life, we must consistently live well in the moment, regularly review our goals and values, have a vision of where we hope to be ten years from now, foresee predictable obstacles, and correct course.

Ask anyone, at any age, how old they are and where they will be when they are [blank] years old. For example:

Q: How old are you?

A: 17

Q: *Where will you be when you are 27 and what are you doing to make sure you will be the best you can possibly be at 27?*

Q: *How old are you?*

A: 65

Q: *Where will you be when you are 75 and what are you doing to make sure you will be the best you can possibly be at 75?*

This simple question opens up an immediate reaction, a world of thought, and some profound clarity. We all have fears and assumptions about age. We have bad habits and wasted time that, if viewed within the framework of this question, become very clear. Choices and trajectory become evident. The BIG purpose of this question is to stand in this moment and from a 10- years-from-now view, see where your current actions are leading you.

The Decade Time Pyramid

If this concept of your life being broken down into decades and quarters of hours seems crazy or obsessive, let me assure you, it does not need to be. It is simply a practical framework for making sure you are using the law of the compound effect in each moment. We all want to look back 10, 20, 30, 40, 50, 60 years from now with NO regrets and many rich experiences to reflect on. There is nothing like knowing you have made a meaningful impact in this life to fill your heart with joy and gratitude.

In order to assure our life is being well lived, we need to have perspective of the short and long term. We need to stay present to the moment, the only place we can take action. Of course, we need little pauses to gain perspective of where we are at and where we are going. Then we must get back to living in the moment. In companies, these are looked at as a schedule of the day/week and monthly/quarterly/semi-annual/annual goals and assessments. Why would we treat our one and only precious life as less important than a successful company?

Failing to plan is planning to fail.
— Benjamin Franklin

A very practical example of a moment of pause to assess where we are at in relationship to time is when I am in a one-hour bodywork session. As a session kicks off, we connect, communicate, assess, consider a course of action, work, and stay present and in discovery mode. I also check the clock against what we have accomplished and what we still need to get done in order to assure the very best and most complete outcome possible.

This is not different from taking my four babies to the mall, all by myself, when they were little. I made a plan the night before and packed accordingly. When the sun rose, one foot in front of the other, I had to stay present and stick to the plan while correcting course as needed. Imagine just getting four babies out of their 5-point harnessed car seats, into the stroller, through the parking lot, and into the building safely. I am a pretty flexible and easy-going person, but being responsible for the safety of four little ones that could run out into traffic or fall on their heads took strategy!

Rules and preparation became HUGE, but even greater was paying attention in the moment. Getting out and having fun experiences was almost as important as our safety to me. Dang! I got tough! It was no longer about what was fair and being willing to think about it. Nope! If you ask any one of my kids, "What are your mom's #1, 2, 3, and 4 rules?" They will all, no doubt, give you the same answer, "STICK TOGETHER!" I am sweet, easy-going, and always set out to have fun, but break that rule, and we are going home immediately and without Chick-fil-A, a train ride, or a scoop of Häagen-Dazs! I do not care who cries, screams, or kicks! Simple as that! Have a plan, set parameters, review at times, and, above all, pay attention and be willing to follow through with the hard parts!

While talking about living a strong life where we get better and stronger with the wisdom and experiences of each decade, it would be a huge oversight not to clearly address how important it is to make sure we are doing what we need to do to live in the best physical body and mind with the least pain and most joy possible. People often ask me how I do it all. Well, knowing my own body and taking great care of it is KEY! One true gift of being an early orthopedic patient is my early understanding that living in pain is difficult and to never take my body and health for granted. I am NOT perfect, but I am consistent with being really good to myself.

We buy new cars every so often because they are machines that break down. If taken care of, our bodies will regenerate, but if not, we break down. Yes, we can buy new knees, just like new shocks in our car, with pretty good outcomes these days, but we cannot buy health. It is something we must choose and nurture through regular self-care, smart exercise, excellent massage and bodywork, clean eating, hydration, plenty of rest, empowering relationships, and great mindset.

We all know it is in times of extreme challenge, physically, mentally, and spiritually, that we grow stronger than we imagined we could be. However, we also know there are things we can do with our moments, hours, days, and months to avoid unnecessary pain and challenges, and to be assured that we will be able to show up and bring our best. Even IF we have well-defined dreams and goals, we will surely still be thrown curveballs! Needless to say, it is not always easy. Unplanned obstacles throw us off course. The world changes around us. We sometimes even get exactly what we thought we wanted, and then realize we do not want it after all! Yikes! I really don't like when that happens! But it happens to the best of us!

I came into this life with the soul of a ballerina and the joints of an early orthopedic patient, so I had multiple reconstructive surgeries by age 16. By my senior year of high school I was sure I wanted to be an orthopedic surgeon. Those guys were the heroes. They made me able to walk without pain and dislocation. I went from excruciating surgeries, painful therapy sessions, and hobbling around on crutches during my freshman and sophomore years of high school, to joining the cheer squad during my senior year.

Imagine my excitement when I learned that the study of muscles, joints, and movement is a whole world of its own called kinesiology. I was hooked! By my senior year of high school I had dug into the AP sciences and gotten my first real gym job at Family Fitness Center in Los Alamitos, California, as a fitness consultant. This entailed giving tours of the facility, selling memberships, and showing people how to use equipment. I figured this would be the perfect college job for a girl who wanted to be an orthopedic surgeon. Needless to say, I took this gig seriously!

My boss, John, was a stickler for reading inspiring books by incredible authors like Og Mandino, James Allan, Napoleon Hill, and Earl Nightingale, to name a few. John was always putting my mindset in check. At the young age of 18, I was guided to life and career management trainings that included everything from deep lessons and conversations, which taught mindset and empowering language, to rock climbing expeditions designed to force you to face your fears and do it anyway. Life, up to that point, fueled me with passion for helping people live their personal best lives.

It was in this sweet decade, back in the 90s, that I discovered that personal trainers were real and not just a Hollywood thing. I was blown away that people would actually pay me to help them do something I loved so much. My roots taught me that each of us has our own unique body, mind, and life mission. There is no "one-size-fits-all." We have to live with our eyes open, our feet on the ground, a vision of the big picture and presence in the moment, and accepting changes in trajectory as quite possibly perfect and not necessarily a failure. It was no failure that I never left the gym to be a surgeon. For me, it was a dream upgrade!

In my second decade, my dreams started coming to fruition. I signed my very first corporate lease for my first personal training company, LifeTime Personal Training. An awesome career that I loved so much was in full swing. With some twists and turns I met and married my best friend, and we had the big family I always dreamed of having (and even at a young age like I'd hoped), still leaving time later for career and travel. We had five children at an early age, just like I wanted! (Yep . . . four became five! When our babies were eight, seven, five-and-a-half, and four years old, we adopted a fifth, whom we affectionately think of as our "most chosen one," and we thank God for her in our lives and family every day).

CAUTION: Just because we get what we always wanted does not mean it is going to be easy. Success requires a delicate balance of patience, persistence, presence, planning, perspective, resetting as needed, and a darn good sense of humor much of the time!

Sometimes, especially when we are going through hard times, planning and goal setting seem like something we will get to when we are through THIS storm. It can be so hard to focus and know where to start. It sometimes seems we just need to get through whatever is currently overwhelming us and then we can see our goals clearly. Oh, if only it were that easy! In reality, if you want to live a bold and courageous life, you have to LEAP—*lead*, *expand*, take *action*, and *play*—into the unknown. You cannot wait for the road map! Just LEAP!

Whether you feel like you are on top of the world, in the eye of the storm, or somewhere in between . . . START HERE AND NOW . . . in this moment, on this day!

Yes, part of living a purpose-driven life is to remember and grow from the lessons in the past, to look around to see what excites you and what turns you off, and to look to the future to shape your hopes and dreams. However, what is imperative if you want to gain traction and enjoy the process is to BE IN THE HERE AND NOW, living YOUR life, rowing YOUR own boat with a hopeful heart and positive beliefs. Embrace your uniqueness and seize the divine opportunities that come your way! Surround yourself with and spread greatness, wherever you go!

> *The only place we have the power to achieve*
> *anything is in THIS moment.*

At the foundation of every session I have with my clients is being fully present, healing hurts, replacing "should do's" with focus-driven "want to's," and shifting from tolerating problems to solving them. Sometimes it feels like we are being controlled by externally imposed barriers—stuck and trapped without a choice. I work within the framework of resolving the mindset of tolerating things and replacing excuses for being stuck with immediate and doable actions and short- and long-term goals. I also work on shifting mindsets to leave my clients empowered to take action and move in the direction of their hopes, health, and dreams.

"Decade thinking" is about realizing that life is long, AND it is short at the same time. This phenomenon is clear when we look backward or forward ten years from wherever we are. Thinking of our lifetime, from being in the moment to having short-, middle-, and long-term perspectives, guides us to make the most of the moments of our life. We begin to get more selective with what we choose to, and not to, spend our time on.

We become invested in solving problems by:

A. Stopping what we are doing immediately if it does not serve our life purpose

B. Reframing the way we look at things so that they become a true positive

110

C. If even after reframing the problem in your mind, it is still a negative but it is more complicated due to certain agreements, then we focus on a phase-out plan somewhere in the immediate days, weeks, months, or year.

Making the most of this one and only, record-breaking, outrageous life of yours, however many days, years, and decades you have, starts here and now.

Yes! Pause, plan, look forward, look around, reflect, but above all—BE HERE NOW—100% with all your heart, mind, body and soul.

Pour into Life!

This is your life . . . your story . . . what are you writing about?

What are the top five core values for your life?

What are your best practices when what you are doing is working?

What are the rituals you follow morning, noon, and night without thought?

What happens if you put them through a "Decade Time Pyramid Review"?

Where are your daily actions leading you in the long term?

Let me suggest that from both a physical and a mindset perspective, you approach this little thing we call life by ditching the "should do's" from the get go! The life you were born to live is not about what you or others think you "should do." It would be easy and boring if we came with a roadmap that told us where to go, what to do, and how to do it so that we never have to experience failure. It seems so cliché, but life truly is a journey, and when we walk through it, "should-ing all over our path," we miss the joy and perfection of the ups, downs, ins, and outs that make us who we are.

Your best practices include humbly considering the advice of worthy mentors, but they also begin with some quiet listening to your true self—your own bones, tissues, heart, mind, and soul purpose.

What are you uniquely gifted at?

What makes your soul sing?

What hurts you and makes you want to rise up and make change?

More importantly what are the things you know you must do to be living in integrity with your life's mission?

What are the things you are currently doing that from this deeper level do not really fit and need to be ditched, either immediately or somewhere in the funnel of your next week, month, year, or decade?

Please, do not live a life of "should-ing" on yourself and others. Let what is at this moment be perfect because it is where are you are now and it is the only launchpad for where you are going. Start right now with a heart full of gratitude and unwavering commitment to living a happy and impactful life.

Are you ready? It is super simple. We can "but-but-but" and "should do" all over it, but it truly breaks down into this one simple word . . .

Time

What are you going to do, and not do, with your precious time? This question applies whether you are struggling and full of great reasons why your life is not the way you want it to be, your body hurts, your bank account is upside-down, your key relationships are bankrupting your soul, OR you are thriving, leading, loving, experiencing physical well-being, financial wealth, and great purpose in life.

We all have the same number of hours in a day and minutes in an hour—are you ready for this? For better or for worse, we all have the same amount of choice on how we use it.

Strong living is an individual process of truly living versus walking around, giving power to our excuses (no matter how valid they seem), and copying those who are seemingly prettier, stronger, richer, and smarter than us. A fulfilling life is one that requires your eyes to be open. It demands you be in touch with your own pulse. What makes YOU work? The bigger the dream, the more intention and structure you will need to funnel and guide your actions.

P.S.—My Grandma's golden heart lives on because she truly lived and loved intentionally, and left a very special legacy. Now it is our turn!

ACTION STEP

A few mindset questions for life:

How long do you think you will live?

How many decades do you have to enjoy that life?

What are the predictable health threats that if not addressed could rob you of quality of life and optimal performance?

What are the unique gifts that you love to share?

What do you want your life story to be about?

Where will you be in 10 years from now?

What are you doing right now to make this decade your best yet?

How are you treating your body? Is self-care a significant part of your daily rituals?

What ONE totally doable action can you commit to STOPPING right now that will give you the most positive bang for your buck and if consistent will have an increasingly positive effect on where you are 6 months, 1 year, 2 years, 5 years, 7 years, 10 years from now?

What ONE totally doable thing can you commit to STARTING right now that will give you the most positive bang for your buck and if consistent will have an increasing positive effect on where you are 6 months, 1 year, 2 years, 5 years, 7 years, 10 years from now?

114

ABOUT LISA BERMAN

Whatever your special gift,
it is your responsibility to spread it in the world.
It is not about how long you live but about how well you live
and the impact you leave on people and the planet.

— Lisa Berman

Lisa Berman is a graduate of the California College of Physical Arts and a licensed massage therapist, who maintains an active professional affiliation with the American Massage Therapy Association. She is also a certified personal trainer through the American Council on Exercise and a certified Pilates instructor through the BASI Pilates Academy where she began her study with the CTT course in 1996. She went on to complete the master course and was selected as an honored Torch Mentee, all under the direct instruction of world-renowned master Pilates instructor, Rael Isacowitz.

Most recently Lisa has dug into the study of functional neurology with Z-Health where she has completed certifications as a Movement Re-education Specialist, Integration Specialist, Performance Specialist, and

Exercise Therapy Specialist. She is currently continuing to seek that top 1% edge in a two-year master trainer program.

Lisa has engaged in thousands of private training and hands-on bodywork sessions over the past two decades and enjoys her "time in the trenches," guiding clients from all walks of life to live healthier, happier, and more empowered lives. She has led teams of trainers, Pilates instructors, and massage therapists, writes for various publications, and speaks to groups encouraging a wellness approach to exercise and life. She continues to work with a private clientele and directs her team of fitness and wellness experts at her studio, 333 FIT in Corona Del Mar, California.

Lisa Berman, LMT, CPT, CPL

CEO, Personal Best Living, LLC
Owner, Studio 333 FIT
www.bermanfitness.com
Instagram: @lisa.berman
Facebook: @LisaBermanFitness

CHAPTER 8

LIVING BETWEEN EXTREMES

by Kelli O'Brien Corasanti

"We should go to Hawaii," they said.

"Hawaii?" I asked nervously. "Really?"

"Yes!" they shouted. "Let's go to Hawaii!"

And that was how the decision was made.

My kids (who at the time were 5, 8, and 10 years old), and I were discussing the possibility of going on a trip. It was my idea. Their father and I had separated, and we had just moved into another house. I wanted them to feel good about the transitions happening in our lives, and I wanted them to feel connected to each other and to the family despite the fact that the marriage was ending. At the time, the overarching goal in my mind was finding a way for the four of us to work together as a team. The changes in our lives were creating uncertainty, and I wanted us to pull together, to figure out a way to bond ourselves into this new formation of a family. I knew we needed a goal, and going on a trip seemed like something that would serve all of those purposes.

Of course, I did not foresee them suggesting Hawaii!

I was a newly single mom with a part-time job and 3 children to feed. The only savings I had was in the coin jar on the kitchen counter—$16.32 of loose change. I could not afford to take us 30 minutes down the road on a bus, so forget across the country to Hawaii. How would we ever be able to get there?

When I asked the question, "Where would you like to go?" I thought they might suggest the beach or Cape Cod, some place closer and much more reasonable, in my opinion. I had a vision of taking a few months to save, then heading off on a trip where we could create memories and have a good time together.

That was my idea, but they had another one.

When they said, "Hawaii," my initial reaction was to tell them no. My mental list quickly filled with all the reasons that Hawaii would be impossible—the expense, the time it takes to get there, missing school, and so on. Fortunately, I did not share my thoughts out loud because I quickly realized that this trip was supposed to be "ours" not "mine." I wanted to show them that when they set a goal, they could achieve it. I wanted them to learn how to rely on each other and to work together. I wanted them to feel the excitement that comes when you work hard to earn something. Plus, I wanted them to know that despite the changes we were experiencing, we were going to be okay. If I told them no, it would negate all of the lessons I wanted them to learn.

And so, with a lump of fear in my throat and a sinking feeling in my stomach, I opened my mouth and said, "Okay. Hawaii, it is!"

What followed was four years of making the impossible, possible! That's right. From that original $16.32 we continued to save, and finally, in 2011, my kids and I went to Maui. The first day we arrived, we stood together on the beach to watch the sunset. With the glow of the fading sun on his shoulders and a proud smile on his face, my son summed up our success and our feeling of accomplishment.

"Wow," he said. "We really did it!"

With that trip, we moved from one extreme to the other. We went from feeling uncertain and afraid about the changes in our lives to feeling successful and accomplished. We went from not knowing what was coming next to taking control and then achieving our goal.

The real success in this story, however, was in the space we lived between those two moments. It was in those four years that we pulled together and made it happen. During those four years, we became a team. We worked together. We created strategies to save money. We shared pictures and stories about our dream, and made plans about what we would do when we got there. The anticipation of the trip gave us hope and excitement, and everything we prepared helped to fan the flame of that emotion.

If you are wondering how we did it, here was our strategy in a nutshell:

1. We collected loose change.

Everywhere we went we looked for change. When we found it, we put it in the loose change bowl on our kitchen counter. It is amazing how much money you can find lying around if you just look for it.

We found coins on sidewalks, change in the cushions of the couch, and quarters that had rolled under the seats in the car. If something cost us $3.04, we would pay with $4.00 and keep the 96 cents to put into our savings bowl.

Every time we filled the bowl, we would have about $100. We would count it and then put it into our savings account at the bank.

People were so enamored with our idea to collect change that many actually donated their own coins to our cause. Several friends, and even my dad, gave us bags and buckets of change to contribute to our mission. Those surprises fed our anticipation and fueled our desire to keep saving.

2. We shared our dream.

I knew it was important to keep the dream alive, so I told the kids to keep their eyes and ears open for anything they heard about Hawaii and to share it with all of us. It was not long before my daughter read a story about Hawaii at school and came home to tell us about it. My other daughter made a sign with the letters of the word, Hawaii, and hung it up in the kitchen, so we could always see it.

We bought a travel book about Hawaii. Each of us looked through it and chose places that we wanted to see. Then we discussed what we were going to do and where we would go when we got there.

We also shared our idea with people who were willing to listen. That way our goal was always present, and the excitement someone else had about it would reignite our own desire to keep working hard toward the goal.

Over four years, we consistently worked together. We shared our dream with others and with each other. In that process, we also bonded to each other in a new way.

It was in that four years that we learned to live with our new life. And eventually, we made it to Hawaii!

Every one of us experiences ups and downs in life. There are times when we are full of despair, and we cannot see our way out of uncertainty, depression, frustration, anxiety, or fear. There are also times when we feel confident, accomplished, successful, and full of joy. Those are the "waves" of life, and every one of us experiences them.

I like to think of those waves in visual terms. Do you remember learning about sine and cosine waves in math or physics? Waves are depicted on a graph with peaks and troughs as seen below:

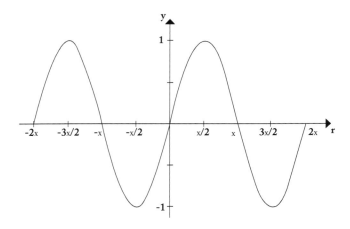

What I want you to notice is that the height of the wave (the peak) is equal to the depth of the wave (the trough).

You may be wondering what this has to do with life, so let me explain.

When you are feeling really down and depressed, you are experiencing the bottom of the wave—the trough. It is really easy to get stuck in that spot—to feel the lows very intensely and to think that you will never get out of them.

But there is no such thing as half of a wave. A wave ebbs and flows. What goes down must come back up. Both extremes are present at all times.

121

In other words, the only reason you can experience depression in life is because you have also experienced the contrasting emotion of happiness and joy. One cannot exist without the other.

Here are some basic ideas to consider:

How high you go and how low you go are what create the extremes of your life.

How high you go and how low you go depend on the intensity of your emotions and how deeply you are able to feel.

How long you stay at any one spot depends on the choices you make.

Once you understand that both types of emotion exist at any given moment and that as intensely as you experience one is as intensely as you will experience the other, then you can begin to make a choice about how you want to LIVE.

Living is what happens between the peaks and troughs. Living is what you do with your life to move through whatever comes your way. Living is what happens when you make choices that move you from moments that do not feel great to ones that feel better. Living is what happens between the two extremes!

So, take a moment right now and ask yourself these questions:

How am I living my life?

Where am I on the continuum of this wave?

Am I stuck?

The reality is that you are not fully living if you are stuck anywhere on the continuum of the wave. A full life happens when there is a continuous flow between ups and the downs. In addition, it simply feels better to be up, so working to find ways to shorten the troughs and extend the peaks is a good strategy.

The next question: how does someone do that?

What follows is a compilation of ideas I formed from my experience of working with people over my past 13 years as a personal trainer and coach.

When people decide to hire a personal trainer, it is because they want to make a change in their life. In some way, they are not happy with where things are right now. Perhaps they want to lose weight or become more toned. Maybe they want to feel fewer aches and pains, or rehabilitate an injury. They might have goals to compete in an event or to improve their scores. They might just want to be healthier. Whatever the reason for them to come, they are there because they have made a choice to make a change.

In some way, every person I have worked with through the years is there because they do not like where they are and they want to do, be, or feel something different. When they come into my studio, it is because they have decided to make a change. Seen another way, you can say they are somewhere in the trough of their wave, and they want to be lifted back up.

Here is what I believe every one of us can do to live our best life. Inevitably, the more we follow these practices, the stronger and more fulfilling a life we will lead.

1.   Take Care of YOU.

I have worked with so many people through the years who take care of everyone around them. They are givers. They give and give and give, and then one day, they realize they are falling apart. Their body is giving out, or they are burned out from life. So many people come in on the downside of their wave, and they are stuck there, trying to figure out how to feel better.

If I could give one piece of advice to anyone wanting to live a stronger life, it would be to take care of YOU first.

When my kids were little, I remember someone telling me the same thing. They said, "When mom isn't doing well, no one is doing well." And that is absolutely the truth. Whether you are a mom or dad, a brother or sister, son or daughter, it is imperative that you take care of YOU. When you do, you will have so much more to give to the world around you.

2. Move More.

Something I have learned from working with people through the years is that it is impossible to move one aspect of our being without moving the others. If we move our body physically, it makes our mind shift. If we have a different mental state, we move our body differently. If we foster our spirit and nurture our emotions, then we begin to think differently. Mind, body, and spirit are all parts of us, and although they are represented in three separate words, they are actually fully connected within us.

Let me give you some examples:

When you are feeling down and you take a walk outside, what happens? Although your problems may not be solved, taking a physical walk allows you to feel more relaxed and to think more clearly.

My mother used to tell me that if I was feeling down, I should get up and move. Sitting and "stewing" (her word) about the problem would not solve it. But cleaning the house, getting outside, and just moving around would make solutions appear and help lift my mood.

There have been countless times through the years that people come into the studio to do a workout and suddenly ended up in tears. That was not because the workout was too hard and they were in physical pain; it was because as soon as they began to move physically, their mental state shifted and their emotions began to flow. Oftentimes they shared a problem they were facing or described emotional turmoil they were experiencing, and it all came to the surface as soon as they began to exercise. Their emotion was a natural result of moving.

What does this mean?

It means that if you want to live a strong life, you must move more physically, challenge yourself more mentally, nurture your spirit more frequently, and allow your emotions to move more easily. Moving more strengthens your body, your mind, and your spirit.

3.   Nurture Your Mindset.

What you feed your mind is exactly what your mind will produce. If you are watching negative news, you will feel negative. If you are thinking negative thoughts, you will feel down. What you consume is what you become. With that in mind, if you want to live a strong life, then you need to develop a consistent routine that feeds positivity into your life.

For me, that consists of daily rituals. Every morning, I get up early enough to enjoy quiet time before my kids wake up. In the peaceful hush of those early hours, I spend time stretching my body, reading something inspiring or motivational, and meditating. I finish with prayers of gratitude.

In the evening, I tuck my girls into bed, stretch a bit more, then spend a few minutes reading something inspirational before turning out the light.

I consider those routines the "bookends" of my day, and I protect that time. I know that the way I start and finish the day will go a long way toward how I live my day.

Where you are in the spectrum of life is directly connected to your mindset. People who are "stuck" in the trough of life are focusing their thoughts and energy on things that do not make their life better. They are focused on what they "don't want" in life.

As Tony Robbins states, "Where your focus goes, energy flows." In other words, the more you concentrate on what you don't want, the more you will get of what you don't want.

The reverse is true as well. As soon as you begin to focus on what you do want, your energy will begin to flow that way. That shift in mindset does not necessarily occur in an instant (although it can). But, typically, it happens over time when you feed your mind more uplifting thoughts and more creative ideas. Consistently nurturing your mindset will help you live a much stronger life.

4. Feed Your Anticipation.

This is a critical piece to living a strong life. Anticipation comes from seeing where you want to go and being excited about getting there. It is the emotion that results from visualizing your dream. Anticipation requires that you have hope. If you are in the depths of despair, hope may seem difficult to find. But if you can find something—anything— to anticipate, then you will begin to shift to a more uplifting place.

The kids and I fed our anticipation of going to Hawaii by surrounding ourselves with items and stories that allowed us to visualize our dream. There were many times when I questioned whether we would ever get there. There were many times when we all wondered if we were going to succeed. What kept us moving was the feeling of excitement and anticipation that we felt every time we dreamt about what was going to happen.

Anticipation does not just happen. You have to feed into it. Visual reminders help to do that. Sharing your dream and ideas with others helps. Closing your eyes and spending time imagining your goal can help. Any of these actions helps fan the emotion. And the more time you spend in that feeling of anticipation, the better you feel.

5. Build a Team.

Many years ago, I was doing an initial consultation with a new client. She was sharing her story with me and described some of the physical challenges she was facing. She told me what she wanted to achieve, and then she said, "I want you to be part of my team."

At first I was surprised. I had not thought about my role as a trainer in quite that way before. But she had a great point. She was developing her own personal wellness team. It consisted of her family, her physician, her massage therapist, and now, me. Each "player" on the team was providing a different component to her plan to heal and be well.

We all need a team if we want to live a strong life. Sharing with others, becoming part of a community, nurturing friendships, developing relationships—all of these things are part of the team we create. Human beings are social creatures. Creating a community of people, including them in your plans, and keeping them apprised of your goals helps to foster relationships and is an important component to living your best life.

6.   Have Faith.

Faith is an often unspoken piece of the puzzle of life. We are so cautious about sharing our beliefs with others for a myriad of reasons that I do not need to outline here. However, I would be remiss if I did not include this as something that I believe is a building block to living a strong life. I am not suggesting that your faith needs to be about any particular religion or spiritual belief. It is about believing in SOMETHING that is bigger than you. It is about recognizing your role in this universe and knowing that in some way, we are all bound together. It is about fostering your spirit and believing in something.

Two years ago, I watched my mother lose her battle with cancer. Not once during those final months did she ever express fear. Not once did she ever get lost in the depression of her illness and what was to come. Not once did she ever feel sorry for herself. She accepted the end of her life with such grace.

A few days before she passed away, I sat on a chair next to her bed. I marveled at how peaceful she seemed and how accepting she was of what was to come. I asked her how she was handling what she was experiencing.

She said, "Kelli, I have faith that it is all going to be okay. If I feel uncertain about what is coming, I just say to myself, 'I can and I will. Just take it one step at a time.'"

On the night she died, she asked my sisters and me to gather around her and sing her favorite hymns. I crawled up on the bed beside her and wrapped my arms around her. Her body was giving up, and she felt so delicate. We sang "Amazing Grace" and "How Great Thou Art." She was weak, but she mouthed the words along with us. I will never forget how content she looked as she smiled and sang along. Not long after that, she took her last breath.

To this day, I am still in awe of the peace and contentment she felt in those last moments. Even as her body failed and she slipped away from us, she continued to lean so strongly on her faith.

She could do that because she had fostered her faith throughout her entire life. Her beliefs held her up from the time she was born until the moment she left this world. One of my mother's greatest gifts to me was demonstrating that living a full life requires you to have faith.

I do not claim to have the answer on how to create that kind of faith in your life. But I do know that it is an important part of living a purposeful and fulfilling life. Find something to believe in and consistently feed that belief. It will see you through it all.

I began this chapter with the story of how my kids and I went to Hawaii, so I want to end with it as well. The story of that trip is a great example for leading a strong life. The extremes my kids and I experienced—from the uncertainty of the change happening in our lives to the success of reaching our goal—are representative of the many extremes that all of us experience in life.

In reality, the world is full of extremes. The sun rises and sets. Waves ebb and flow. There is despair and joy. We are born and eventually we die. However, what I wanted my kids to learn was something I learned along the way as well. Life is what happens between all of those extremes, and how strong you live it depends on each and every choice that you make.

Choose wisely and live strong!

ACTION STEP

What are some of the extremes that
you are currently experiencing in your life?

Do you find yourself stuck in any one place?

Use what you learned in this chapter to write down ONE ACTION STEP
you can take that will move you forward out of your stuck position.
And then go out and DO IT!

About Kelli O'Brien Corasanti

Kelli O'Brien Corasanti is a bestselling author, coach, presenter, and the owner of Studio 8 Fitness, Inc., a personal training and life transformation studio located in Upstate New York. Recently, she co-founded Scriptor Publishing Group, Inc., a publishing company dedicated to helping fitness professionals share their stories and publish their books.

Kelli holds a master's in counseling education and certifications in personal training, TRX, and youth fitness. She is the author of *Kelli's Quips: Happy Thoughts for Busy People* and *Finding My Way Back to Me: A Journey of Self-Discovery*. She has also co-authored several books, including, most recently, the Amazon bestseller, *Author University*.

She is a Platinum Level Coach for the Todd Durkin Mastermind Group where she provides business and personal development coaching for fitness professionals around the world. She also runs a life-coaching program called Finding My Way Back to Me.

Kelli is the recipient of the Accent on Excellence Award for her work in her community, and she presents locally and nationally on topics having to do with health, wellness, mindset, and performance. In 2013, she was honored to be a presenter for the first TedXUtica program.

Kelli's life purpose is to create, motivate, support, and inspire others to achieve their goals, and she does that with enthusiasm in whatever she pursues. However, she finds her greatest joy in the time spent with her family—Graeme, Marcus, Katie, and Kira—and their exuberant and extremely loveable dog, Cody.

Kelli O'Brien Corasanti, MS

Owner, Studio 8 Fitness

www.studio8fitness.com

Facebook: @Kelli.O.Corasanti

CHAPTER 9

CREATING A WORLD-CLASS MINDSET: HOW TO CONTROL YOUR OWN FATE

by Greg Justice

"I'm sorry, but I just don't think you're college material."

Even though those words were uttered more years ago than I care to admit, I still remember the feeling of shock that echoed through my body when I met with my high school counselor. After all, this was a woman who was paid to give me the steps I needed to achieve my goals.

Who was she to tell me that I was not good enough for college?

But a funny thing happened after that fateful meeting—her words started rolling around in my mind. Even though I applied and got into college, I could not shake her oh-so-polite suggestion that I consider something other than going to college.

So, what ended up happening once I was actually in school?

I would like to say that I ended up proving my high school guidance counselor wrong as soon as I stepped on campus. That I not only rocked my first semester but came back to my old high school to slam my transcript on her desk and laugh in her face.

Unfortunately, that is not exactly how it went down.

When You Leave Your Fate in the Hands of Others

Blame it on being young, but I actually ended up believing in what my guidance counselor pointed out—I just was not good enough for college.

So, when my first semester rolled around, I was too scared to put in the work. Things seemed too hard. The other students around me, who seemed to have no problem understanding lessons or handing in their papers on time, intimidated me.

I struggled, and I struggled hard. In fact, after my sophomore year, I was not exactly surprised to end up with a 1.4 GPA.

Yup, you read that right—a 1.4 GPA!

I knew something had to change; after all, if I did not improve my grades, I would end up getting kicked out of school. I cannot put my finger on the exact moment I knew I had to change, but I finally was honest with myself . . .

"I can't do this anymore."

I decided that if I was really going to do well in school—and really apply myself—I needed to focus on something that I was passionate about. The classes I was sitting through did not stimulate me or prompt me to learn. If I was going to turn my life around, I needed to find something that connected with me as a person.

And that is when I found my passion—exercise science.

Fast-forward three years later—I was finishing on the President's List and graduating with a 4.0 GPA.

Think this is a crazy success story? That this is the kind of thing you will only find in a Disney movie?

Fortunately, I am a testament to the fact that anyone can turn their life around. No matter what goals you have, no matter what you are pursuing, you have every capability to make it happen.

The only difference between where you are now and where you are going to end up is that you have to connect to these three things:

1. **Inspired Motivation**

2. **Visualization**

3. **Belief**

I am going to walk you through what each of these points mean—and how you can unleash them in your own life.

After all, the only one in charge of your destiny—is you!

Inspired Motivation: Creating a Passion That Burns

At first glance, the phrase "inspired motivation" might seem a little, well, redundant. Aren't inspiration and motivation the same thing?

Not necessarily. Let's break down each word:

- **Motivation** is about psyching yourself up to do something, whether it is cleaning up around the house or making the decision to go back to school.

- **Inspiration** means to be in the spirit of that something; so if you are planning on going back to school, you really feel the drive, excitement, and determination to complete that goal.

Right away, we can see the main difference between motivation and inspiration—motivation is about **doing** while inspiration is about **feeling**. Inspiration is like the gas in your car while motivation is the act of putting the pedal to the metal.

Inspired motivation is what you need to propel your goals forward. I can guarantee that once you are in this frame of mind, nothing can stop you from achieving what you want. I like to joke that when you are in that frame of mind, you do not have a dream, the dream has you.

For many people, however, achieving this frame of mind can be difficult because they cannot identify what their particular passions are. It is not surprising. Our lives are set up in such a way that it is easy to get caught up in the day-to-day. Between commuting back and forth to work, running errands, and paying bills, it is no wonder that by the end of the day, we are too busy dreaming of getting a good night's sleep.

Not exactly the best setup for discovering our inner passions!

But what exactly is passion—and how can you connect to yours?

In the dictionary, passion is defined as "a strong inclination to an activity that is self-defining, that a person loves, finds important and in which regular time and energy are invested." In other words, a passion feels authentic to who you are as a person. If you are an artist, your passion is painting or sculpting. If you are athletic, your passion might be going for a run during cool early mornings.

Over the past decade, the field of psychology has taken an interest in passion. A number of studies have been conducted on the subject and have subsequently led to the publication of professional papers that have identified two types of passion: **harmonious** and **obsessive**. The difference between the two can be profound—harmonious passion is in-tune with your life and your goals while obsessive passion feels like it consumes you. Ideally, you want to land on the harmonious side of the spectrum, as that's the kind of passion that feels the most authentic to who you are as a person.

Visualization: Who Do You Think You Are?

There is an anonymous quote that goes a little like this: "It's not who you are that holds you back, it's who you think you're not."

Quick—picture yourself as the star of a reality TV show. What character would you be? How do you imagine yourself? What kind of conversations are you having with those around you?

If you're like most people, you probably don't have the best image of yourself. And that is okay! We tend to be our own worst critics, especially when it comes to visualizing ourselves interacting with others.

But there are overwhelming psychological and performance benefits that occur when you cast yourself as the star of your own highlight reel. I am not talking about a literal, video-screened version of events, but rather a developing "film" you imagine of yourself, seeing yourself in your head clearly.

Why is visualization so important? Because the human mind cannot distinguish between a real and a visualized experience.

Now picture yourself doing the activities that are most common in your life. Add in a few additional activities that you are trying to master, like a new skill or hobby. In that film, you are cool, calm, and poised: you are talking to your coworkers or friends in a confident manner, and everyone around you is laughing or listening intently to what you have to say. You are going for a run or working out or just getting lost in some type of physical activity—and you look peaceful and focused while you are doing it. No matter what you are trying to picture, make sure you imagine the best version of yourself possible—no excuses!

However, make sure you avoid the trap of falling into someone else's highlight reel. A lot of us tend to put pressure on ourselves to be the person we think others want us to be. Whether it is a loved one or a toxic relationship in your life, living according to someone else's highlight reel can be extremely dangerous to your sense of self. After all, how can you achieve your own fate when living by someone else's highlight reel?

Keep your own highlight reel playing, and keep it in focus. Allow yourself to feel grateful for and proud of the moments that you're playing back in your own head. When we give ourselves permission to feel happy and grateful, we're much more likely to pursue the activities and moments that led to those emotions—even if they were only the product of visualization.

With practice, your highlight reel can become more than just a reel in your mind. You can authentically experience what you are imagining, even with sounds and smells, as long as you get into the realistic nitty-gritty of the whole.

You Gotta Believe!

After I finished graduate school, I was determined to put my degree to good use. So, I decided to do something that had never been done before—I was going to open Kansas City's first personal training studio. Keep in mind that this was the mid 1980's; aerobics classes were just becoming a nationwide trend, so the concept of personal training was still relatively new (especially in the Midwest!).

Since my personal training business was such big news, several local media outlets interviewed me, including a famous radio personality who had a pretty sizeable listening audience. I remember sitting there, excitedly chatting to him about how my personal training business had the potential to completely change Kansas City. I could see him staring back at me, mulling over something in the back of his mind.

Then he came out and said what he was thinking, all in front of what was possibly an audience of thousands of listeners: "A business like yours is never going to make it in Kansas City."

Wow. I mean, it does not get any more blunt than that!

Rather than be cowed by his opinion, I decided to press on with opening my personal training business. I was not about to let anyone tell me that my dream was not worthwhile to pursue. I had such an intense belief and passion for my personal training business that no one could tell me no.

And you know what? This May (2017), we are celebrating AYC's 31st anniversary in business!

When you have an unshakeable belief in your mission—whether it is to start your own business, lose weight, or move to a completely new city—you will feel the kind of confidence that just cannot be rivaled by anything on this earth. This confidence stems from belief—the almost fanatical understanding that what you are doing is your life's purpose.

Truly believing in what you are doing is key to creating your own destiny. When you do not have that unshakeable belief in yourself, it becomes far too easy for others to tell you what they think about your goals. Soon, you find yourself listening to others a little more. You start giving their opinions and criticisms more space in your head.

Pretty soon, it is all you can listen to—and eventually, those negative criticisms and opinions undermine your confidence to the point where you consider giving up on your dream.

That is exactly why it is important to connect with and grow the sense of belief in yourself that you are doing the right thing, that you are accomplishing what you were born to do in this life. You want the kind of belief that drives you forward in your darkest hours when it seems like it is just too hard to accomplish what you would like to do.

Of course, there is this classic problem: knowing you need to create a sense of belief and purpose is one thing; actually doing it is quite another. You have probably already given space to criticisms and feedback in your mind, so there are some hesitations already holding you back. If you are not exactly feeling confident in your abilities to achieve your goals, what can you do?

This is where I like to point out that building belief—and ultimately becoming successful—comes down to the **three Cs: confidence, courage**, and **commitment**.

I like to use the visual of a triangle with confidence at its base. Courage and commitment are built on confidence. Without confidence, it becomes difficult to give yourself permission to be brave. It becomes even harder to give yourself the drive necessary to accomplish those goals, especially when other people are telling you no.

Confidence is the quality that motivates you to accept and accomplish what might otherwise seem too difficult or impossible. But how do you build confidence when you feel like you do not have enough?

Glad you asked because here are a few tips that I use myself to build unshakeable confidence:

1. Whether it is in your business or your personal relationships, always do what is expected of you . . . and then some. Don't be the person who just gets by. Go above and beyond to prove yourself to everyone around you.

2. Stay focused on yourself and what you can control. As soon as you start comparing yourself to others, you will undermine your confidence and sense of belief. Just do your very best, and everything else will take care of itself.

3. Reward your daily victories, no matter how small they might seem. Write down everything you have accomplished, as they serve as confidence builders for when you're feeling particularly low.

4. Forgive yourself for any setbacks or mistakes you experience on your way to accomplishing your goals. Don't dwell on your mistakes; just accept that they happened and move forward.

5. Keep a feedback journal. Record your thoughts right after a big meeting or performance to see if you can identify any moments when you didn't feel particularly confident. Once you have identified those moments, you will know where you need to do the most work.

6. Know your own self-confidence builders. What works for some might not work for others. If you feel confident after a pep talk with a trusted mentor or always feel a burst of confidence when you talk with others, identify what those confidence builders are and build them into your daily routine as much as possible.

7. Use powerful affirmations as part of your self-talk. Instead of saying, "I want" or "I hope," use phrases like "I am" or "I will." It might not seem like the biggest change, but trust me—it really works for building unshakeable confidence!

In addition to building your sense of confidence, make sure you are using the visualization and motivational techniques to create clear, challenging, and achievable goals. When you combine these techniques with your newfound sense of confidence, you will find that you have the drive and courage needed to move forward with your life—and achieve your fate!

Your Fate Is in No One Else's Hands But Your Own!

Before I leave you to build your own destiny, I want to share with you a question that I get asked a lot during my speaking tours and seminars:

"What happens when a loved one does not understand your dream?"

Your family members and friends provide the support and love you need to pursue your dreams, even when the rest of the world is telling you no. That is probably why, when a member of this pivotal circle does not believe in you, it can feel absolutely devastating.

Believe me, I have been there before.

In fact, my beautiful wife—one of the most supportive and nurturing people I have ever met in my life—was not exactly on board with my ideas to open Kansas City's first personal training studio. She was not as blunt as the radio DJ, but she did express skepticism over my dream.

She would say to me, "Are you really sure that people are going to pay you for that?"

But you know what was the difference between my wife and all those other people who were telling me no? My wife understood that I had a dream and that I was going to do everything in my power to accomplish that dream.

So, even though she did not understand my dream, even though she may have thought it was a little crazy—she still supported me. And that, my friends, makes all the difference between someone who is a naysayer, and someone who supports your dreams.

No matter which type of person is present in your life, just remember this key fact: **you alone are responsible for your fate.** Not your spouse. Not your parents. And certainly not your high school guidance counselor. You alone have the tools and abilities needed to accomplish the things you have always wanted for yourself.

The next time you have a quiet moment, I recommend sitting back, relaxing, and truly thinking about the things you want for yourself. What truly connects with you? What makes you feel incredibly passionate? What have you always wanted to do for yourself but just haven't found the confidence necessary for accomplishing it?

No matter what that might be, I want you to visualize it in your mind's eye. Truly connect with that goal. Believe that you're capable of achieving it—because you are. Use the tips and advice I've given to propel your journey forward.

Your fate is waiting—and only you can achieve it!

ACTION STEP

Close your eyes and spend a few minutes visualizing your goals. What do you want to achieve? What are you passionate about? If you had all the tools you needed, what would you want to do in your life?

After you have a good picture in your mind, take some time to write down your dreams and thoughts in a journal. Refer back to them often, and you will be amazed at how you move forward toward achieving them.

About Greg Justice

Training veteran Greg Justice didn't just get in on the leading edge of an emerging industry, he helped create it. Opening the first personal training studio in Kansas City, Justice has, over the years, laid the groundwork for countless others to follow.
— Shelby Murphy, Editor, PFP Magazine, May 2009

Greg Justice, MA, is a bestselling author, speaker, fitness entrepreneur, and was inducted into the National Fitness Hall of Fame in 2017. He opened AYC Health & Fitness, Kansas City's Original Personal Training Center, in May 1986. Today, AYC specializes in onsite corporate wellness, personal and small-group training.

Greg is the co-founder and CEO of the National Corporate Fitness Institute (NCFI), a certifying body for fitness professionals, and the co-founder of Scriptor Publishing Group.

Greg holds a master's in HPER (exercise science) (1986) and a bachelor's in health and physical education (1983) from Morehead State University, Morehead, KY.

He has been actively involved in the fitness industry for more than three decades as a club manager, owner, personal fitness trainer, and corporate wellness supervisor. He has worked with athletes and non-athletes of all ages and physical abilities, and served as a conditioning coach at the collegiate level. He worked with the Kansas City Chiefs, during the offseason, in the early 1980s, along with professional baseball, soccer, and golf athletes.

Greg has authored 14 books, writes articles, and contributes to many publications including, *Men's Fitness*, *Women's Health*, *Prevention*, *Time*, *US News & World Report*, *New York Times*, *IDEA Fitness Journal*, and *Corporate Wellness Magazine*. For more information, please visit:

Greg Justice, MA

AYC Health & Fitness

aycfit.com

gregjustice.com

Facebook: @GregJustice1

CHAPTER 10

OVERACHIEVE FOR
THE LIFE YOU WANT

by Ralph Roberts

M y grandfather was the first black police officer in our town. He taught me how to overachieve. He inspired me to be different because the different ones always end up being successful. He inspired me to take the road less traveled.

To him, "overachieving" meant working toward a goal that no one else was making the effort to pursue. It meant working late and arriving early. It meant doing the work, even when no one was watching. It meant challenging yourself, each and every day, to do the right thing and make the right decision.

With that background, you can understand why washing strangers' sweaty socks and folding gym towels was not what I envisioned for myself as part of my future job. After all, before that I had spent 10 years pursuing a successful professional baseball career. For seven of those years I pitched for the Atlanta Braves and relished in the perks of being a professional athlete. For the last three years of my career, I played for the Amarillo Dillas, leading the professional minor league baseball team to three consecutive championships before I retired in 2011.

Baseball had always been a part of my life. In high school, I was an All-American and State MVP athlete. I went on to attend Lenoir Community College and worked hard academically as well as on the baseball field. I can still remember times when we were at the bottom of the ninth, bases loaded, and there was a 3–2 count. I can hear the voice in my head asking, "What are you going to do? Are you going to swing, or are you going to take the pitch?" Life was glorious then.

I grew up in Cherryville, North Carolina, with my grandparents, Ralph and Betty Roberts. My parents were divorced when I was 5 and my brother was 4. My father was devastated after my mother left us, so my brother and I moved in with our grandparents for stability. My father ended up moving just a few miles away. Our relationship never wavered, but we continued to live with our grandparents.

My grandparents were the best. When I think about all the sacrifices they made for us, it brings me to tears. They were two hardworking people who had already raised their kids and were choosing to take on two more. It was very hard for my dad, but I somehow understood his emotion as well as the sacrifice it took to accept help while he got on his feet.

One trait my grandparents encouraged in us was to possess a strong work ethic, to overachieve in all that we do. I will never forget the day my grandfather walked into our home and told my brother, Wesley, and me that he needed a second to speak with us. Of course, we dashed over to our grandmother and begged her to tell us what was wrong.

She calmly responded, "Today is a big day in our house."

The suspense was excruciating for two adolescent boys.

My grandfather was a respected figure in our community. As the eldest of 12 children, he grew up looking after his siblings. When he asked to marry my grandmother, her father refused because he didn't have a job, so he worked hard and proved his worthiness.

On this day, my grandfather revealed to my brother and me that he was going to be the first black police officer in Cherryville. When he revealed this news, he concluded with a quote that I hold in my heart till this day. "Overachieve for the life that you want, son," he said. "If you put in the work, no one can take it away from you, especially if you are living right and your purpose is bigger than you."

More than 20 years have passed since my grandfather spoke those words to me, and I still remember them as clearly as when I was 14. His words pushed me to become the father, leader, and fitness professional I am today.

I was blessed with a natural athletic ability that allowed me to excel in sports. My father was a tremendous athlete and received a football scholarship to Mars Hills University. However, I never thought about my athleticism too much. It was who I was. Being the only kid from my neighborhood on the baseball team ate at me at times, but my mentality was always focused on one goal—to make my family proud. If I overachieved, I could make them proud. If I could make them proud, I could be proud. Not only did I want to be a champion on and off the field, but I also wanted respect—from my team, my opponents, and even the neighborhood kids.

In 1998, my high school baseball team was vying for the state championship title for the second consecutive year. Ultimately, we became champions again, but it was not the MVP award of the season, the coveted championship ring, or even being featured on the front page of the local paper that made me feel like a winner. Rather, it was the embrace from my grandfather and grandmother after the game that gave me a sense of triumph. When my grandmother said, "Son, I am so proud of you," I felt invincible. Even still, on the inside, I knew I could still achieve more. For most overachievers, an inner fire invariably ignites you. That fire could be the person that says you will never make it, or it could simply be you wanting to continue to get better.

I was drafted by the San Diego Padres out of high school, but I turned the offer down to remain on the East Coast. My freshman year at Lenoir Community College, I was drafted by the Tampa Bay Devil Rays; then by the Arizona Diamondbacks my sophomore year. But neither felt right. I could have accepted $225,000 for just signing my name, but I followed my heart to the University of North Carolina at Chapel Hill, where I would later sign with the Atlanta Braves.

The day I signed with the Atlanta Braves, all I needed to do was throw 90 mph. Within just five throws, topping out at 94 mph, I became a Brave. Ever since I was a kid, batting with tennis balls with the neighborhood kids at Freedom Park, I knew I wanted to be a professional baseball player. I worked hard to get there. I treated my body like a temple, disciplined myself, and made sure I was always number one.

Life as a professional athlete was amazing. However, I was not focused. I was just coasting on my success and not using it for good. Then, in 2011, it came to an end. For 10 years, I had committed my life to baseball. I did not have anything left to prove, and I was only giving 90 percent. I wanted to walk away when I could make the choice. An injury or release would have devastated me. That is when I knew it was time to put my cleats away. I was ready to see what was next.

A part-time, off-season position at a prestigious health club in Amarillo, Texas, turned into a full-time job working behind the desk. I was grateful to have a job that allowed me to work in the fitness industry and be able to stay in shape. It seemed like a sensible transition from professional sports—at the same time, it was also when I found myself washing strangers' sweaty socks and folding gym towels—so while it was sensible, it was a long shot from overachieving.

I eventually worked my way up from front desk supervisor to assistant director, and now I am the director of personal training at the Downtown Athletic Club. However, for that first year, I was complacent. I procrastinated. There was a void, and it was not from falling out of the spotlight. It was from a lack of overachieving. I was neglecting the person my grandparents raised me to be. I knew that I was settling. What I soon realized was that I did not have to be a professional athlete to overachieve. My grandparents instilled in me a drive to overachieve at anything I set out to accomplish. All I needed was a little push and a reminder of who I was.

That push came at my birthday dinner. I mentioned to a colleague that I was interested in earning the ISSA (International Sports Sciences Association) certification. He scoffed at the idea of me becoming a nationally certified personal trainer. That was all the incentive I needed. It was like a fire, and it was on. That night, I bought the study material and began my journey.

After dedicating every ounce of energy into four months of intense studying, I had no choice but to dominate the certification test. I had never invested this amount of time into anything except baseball, and it felt right. I was confident this was the path I was meant to take. Night after night, I would ask myself, "Is this worth it? Should I move back home or continue working at the front desk?" Those were the easy ways out, and that was the appeal. They were easy. But all of the time I devoted to my goal was worth it when I read a word on my certification results—"Congratulations." I'd passed. I did not celebrate with a party, toast, or dinner though. I celebrated by calling my family—the people who got me here.

Life as a nationally certified personal trainer commenced the next day, and it was a rocky start. In my first week, three clients passed out. The frustration, fear, and sense of failure that rushed through my brain were enough to make me want to quit, but instead, I returned to my why: why did I want to become a nationally certified personal trainer in the first place? I wanted to transform my clients, physically and mentally. I wanted to make their lives better. That is my why, my purpose.

Soon, I was training more than 40 hours a week, leading group trainings on weekends, and asking friends to spread the word about Ralph Roberts Training. A few months later, I reached out to a local news station about presenting an exercise segment. I knew they had another trainer in mind, so I created a game plan to make myself stand out. I partnered with a local marketing agency that was already doing the marketing for the Downtown Athletic Club. I did not have the money to pay them, so I made a deal. I would train their employees in return for marketing and consulting.

It paid off. I will never forget walking into a local restaurant after my first segment aired, ready to devour every greasy dish on the menu. Then the waitress gushed to me, "Ralph, I love your show! But what do you eat off the menu here?" Let's just say I had to rethink my order.

Since I officially started Ralph Roberts Training in 2013, I have joined Todd Durkin's exclusive Mastermind Group, become a respected leader in my community as well as my hometown, and shown my own children what it means to overachieve. The Mastermind has been a game changer. Being a part of this group means being a part of a dream team. The group pushes me, challenges me, and continues to help me be all I can be.

With every bit of success, however, adversity strikes. Nothing hit me harder than the day I lost my father. When my father was just 53, he was diagnosed with stage 4 lung cancer. A routine physical turned into a death sentence: he had only four to six months to live. Several months into his diagnosis, my grandmother called me and passed the phone to my father. I could hear the exhaustion in his voice. He told me he was tired of fighting the cancer, and he didn't want me to be upset with him for giving up. He said I had made him proud. I promised him I would continue to do my best.

I entered my office that morning, I shut the door and immediately collapsed, flooding the floor with tears. I was angry with my father for not fighting harder, for not fighting to be there for the birth of my first son. But how could I be mad at him? How could I blame him for wanting to give up? The cancer had spread throughout his body, and his organs were shutting down. He was in pain and yearned for relief. After hours of prayer, I picked myself up and reminded myself of the man my father wanted me to be.

My father's death could have derailed me from my path. But it didn't. It challenged me. With the new year, I became laser-focused, almost obsessed, with becoming a top fitness professional. I began to develop some strategies that would help me be my best. I challenged myself, and once again, I began to overachieve.

Overachieving and You

What does "overachieve" mean to you?

To some, it means doing a little extra, working a little harder. To me, overachieve means challenging myself while others are doing nothing, always going above and beyond, and as my mentor, Todd Durkin says, constantly giving . . . "and then some."

152

The strategies I practice help me to always do my best. Every day, I try to follow these seven steps:

1. Mirror Check

Every morning and every night I give myself a mirror check. A mirror check is when you reflect on your day and your life and ask your mirror image, "Did you do the best you can? Did you stay focused on your bigger picture? How do you become a better you? Did you overachieve for the life you want?" I reflect upon the day ahead as well as my life in general, asking myself if I am doing the best I can and overachieving for the life I want.

2. Prioritize

The key to overachieving is prioritizing. In my eyes, I must make sure my family is first. As a close friend of mine advised, "You have to take care of home and everything else will follow." My family always comes first. The closer you get to your bigger picture, the bigger the adversity will be to try and slow you down. Surround yourself with thoroughbreds who not only hold you accountable but are there to help you be the best you.

3. Take Action

Action is our ally; don't sit idly by. We can sit here and put on the "poor me" attitude, or we can take action. Complacency is our enemy and action is our ally. Instead of safely hiding behind the desk at the Downtown Athletic Club, I chose to take a risk and become a nationally certified personal trainer. What risks do you need to take in order to create your success? Remember your dream is not big enough unless it scares you. Sometimes we have to take a leap of faith to achieve our dreams.

4. Develop Consistency

Another key to overachieving is consistency. Every week, I consistently share three workout tip videos on social media, publish two blogs on my website, and post a Monday Motivation video as well as a Weekly Reflection video. If you create a solid plan and stick to it, you will have the opportunity to create exceptional experiences for people every day. If it were easy, trust me, everyone would be doing. The road less traveled always leads to success if you are consistent and pay attention to detail.

5. Live Your Purpose

Do a deep dive and find your calling. You too can act like a world-class citizen and discover your purpose. Knowing your why keeps you focused and on track. Practice what you preach and not only choose to get 1% better in everything that you do but also create exceptional experiences for everyone that you come across. The power that you can have in just a simple hello could change the world. Remember, it is your dream. It is your bigger picture.

6. Challenge Yourself

Always work hard to be your best. It isn't about competing with other people. It is about competing with yourself. Your journaling, daily readings, as well as treating yourself as "world-class" can help with this process. Challenge yourself and treat your body the way it deserves. Overachieve for the life that you want and challenge yourself to be nothing less than great.

7.   Separate Yourself

"Separate yourself from the pack." I can hear my grandmother telling me that right now. If you want something, work for it. Challenge yourself today for the life that you want. Be different and make yourself stand out. Becoming a champion is not about just standing at the mountaintop; it is remembering the journey that got you there to be the best you possible.

Over the years, I developed these seven daily steps based on the words of my grandparents as well as the lessons I gained from my career as a professional baseball player and personal trainer. I encourage you to create your own set of steps and strive to uphold them every day—and then some.

A few months after my father's passing, I began to regain a sense of normalcy and routine. As I left my morning show at the news station, I received a unique phone call. Someone from my high school asked me to give the commencement speech at the school's 2016 graduation ceremony. Days later, I learned that I would also throw the first pitch at my high school's baseball field, on Ralph Roberts Day. Other than playing a friendly game of catch with my eldest son, I had not thrown a baseball off a mound in three years.

When I arrived at my childhood home in Cherryville, I immediately swiped my Braves baseball out of my trophy case and went to the backyard to practice. It was like I was once again a young Braves pitcher, and the fence was my catcher. I knew I still "had it" when a frantic neighbor scrambled out of her house with her dog asking about the loud boom.

Before throwing the pitch on Ralph Roberts Day, I stood on the mound and thought about my father and grandfather. I could see my boys looking at me with pride, and I knew they felt the same way I had when my grandfather announced that he become the first black police officer. It is not the recognition that steers you on the path to overachieve, but rather the impact you can make on the people you love. Like my grandfather, I too want my boys to overachieve and find their purpose in life. I want them to dig deep and understand they can achieve success if they put in the work.

As I threw that pitch, I suddenly realized how far I had come. I am a respected leader in the Amarillo, Texas community and a role model in my hometown. I am a nationally certified personal trainer and recognized fitness professional. I am a father my two boys can look up to, and I know my own father would be proud. And now I can share the lessons my grandparents taught me with all of you.

Overachieve for the life that you want, and challenge yourself to be nothing less than great!

ACTION STEP

What do you need to do to be great?

Maybe you are afraid to stand alone or to take the road less traveled.
Maybe you have lost focus time and time again.
What are you going to do differently?

What is your why?

And what will you do differently to live a life worth telling a story about?

ABOUT RALPH ROBERTS

Ralph graduated from the University of North Carolina at Chapel Hill with a degree in psychology. He joined the Downtown Athletic Club team in Amarillo, TX, in 2008 after concluding a 10-year career in professional baseball. In his baseball career he spent 7 years with the Atlanta Braves organization and 3 with the Amarillo Dillas.

Ralph is a nationally certified personal trainer and a certified TRX trainer. He was recognized nationally when he finished 12th in the *Men's Health* Next Top Trainer contest. In addition, he is a member of Todd Durkin's Platinum Level Mastermind Program, an organization of top fitness professionals in the industry.

You can watch Ralph on his weekly television show, *Workout Wednesday*, on ABC 7 Amarillo. As the fitness correspondent, he showcases workouts you can do from home, as well as a variety of exercises that you can add to your regular workout routine.

In addition to his training business, where he leads his personal training team, he enjoys spending time with his fiancé, Shawna, and his two sons, Bentley and Kamryn. As a former professional athlete, his life is full of helping people in sports and mentoring kids to make the correct choices in sports and in life. He teaches his sons that they do not have to follow in their dad's footsteps; they can live their own lives and create their own legacies.

Ralph Roberts, ISSA CFT

Downtown Athletic Club

www.ralphrobertspersonaltrainer.com

Instagram: @ralphrobertscpt

Facebook: @ralphcpt

67783588R00091